52 Timeless Toys to Knit

Chris de Longpré

Timeless Knits Publications, Kentwood, Michigan, U.S.A.

Copyright © December 2013

Chris de Longpré

ISBN 978-0-9793605-5-8

All rights reserved. No part of this book may be reproduced or transmitted in any form or by any means, electronic or mechanical, including photocopying, recording, or by any other information storage technique, except for the inclusion of brief quotations in an article or review, without express permission of the author.

Photography: Chris de Longpré
Illustrations: Katherine Bates
Book design: Janel Laidman

Timeless Knits Publications, a division of
Knitting At KNoon Designs, LLC
Kentwood, Michigan

e-mail: Chris@TimelessKnitsPublications.com
website: TimelessKnitsPublicactions.com

Printed in the United States by Versa Press, Inc., East Peoria IL

For John

Table of Contents

Introduction	5
Read Me First	6
Materials and Equipment	6
General Instructions	9
Notes, Techniques, and Abbreviations	12
Embroidery Stitches	15

THE PATTERNS

Down Under	19
Crocodile	20
Kangaroo and Joey	23
Kiwi	28
Koala	30
Platypus	32
Flock	35
Blue-footed Booby	36
Flamingo	39
Peacock	42
Penguin	45
Toucan	48
Heartland	51
Cow and Calf	52
Ewe and Lamb	57
Goose and Goslings	61
Hen and Chicks	66
Sow and Piglets	69
Midnight Sun	73
Baby Beluga	74
Moose	76
Polar Bear	79
Puffin	81
Walrus	84
Reef	87
Blue Tang	88
Clown Fish	91
Crab	94
Shark	96
Starfish	100
Serengeti	103
Elephant	104
Giraffe	107
Lion	110
Monkey	113
Zebra	116
Southwest	119
Armadillo	120
Coyote	123
Javelina	126
Lizard	128
Prairie Dog	131
Wetlands	133
Beaver	134
Frog	137
Garter Snake	140
Snail	142
Turtle	144
Woodlands	147
Mouse	148
Owl and Owlets	150
Rabbit	152
Skunk	154
Squirrel	156
Acknowledgements	159

Introduction

Welcome to my happy place! I'd like to share with you the joy I feel every time I create a knitted toy. If you've never knitted a toy, you may be wondering why anyone would. Let me challenge you to make just one knitted toy from this collection. I think you will be surprised by the fun you will have as its personality emerges.

It is amazing to me that, in this age of computerized and battery-powered toys that move, light up, and make sounds, my humble folk toys have enchanted the children in my life (and the grownups, too). There is no end to the smiles they elicit and the imaginative play they inspire.

I'm often asked about the process involved in designing my toys. You may notice that many of the toys in this book share the same, teardrop-shaped body. Turning that shape into a specific animal requires caricature—selecting the features that define the animal and exaggerating them. Note the differences between the elephant and the kiwi. Along with caricature, the shaping is sculptural and very subtle, as evidenced in the faces of the ewe and lamb contrasted with the faces of the cow and calf. It would be possible to create more realism, but much of the charm of these toys is in their simplicity.

Of the 52 patterns included in this book, eleven have been previously published, mostly by my pattern publishing company, Knitting At KNoon Designs, LLC, but also by several other publishers. My design and pattern writing skills have grown in the eight years since I wrote my first toy patterns. I think you will find value added to every previously-published pattern: all can easily be knit in any circular knitting style you prefer and all the designs have been refined to make them the best they can be.

Where is the camel, the manatee, the tiger, the egret, the seahorse, the scorpion, the hedgehog? I know I will receive letters requesting animals not included in this book. Alas, I had to define an endpoint for this project. I fully expect that once you have worked through a part of this collection, you will have the necessary tools to imagine what changes you need to make to create any animal that suits your fancy.

So go ahead—knit some fun!

Chris de Longpré
December 2013

Read Me First

In software there is often a file on the installation disk named, "Read Me First." As the name implies, reading this file before installation or operation of the software will answer a lot of questions and ensure that the software operates properly with the desired effects. Similarly, reading all the material in this section will answer most of the questions you are likely to have when you begin your first pattern from this book, and point you in the right direction for materials and techniques. I do hope you will read it first, or at least familiarize yourself with the contents. Then you will know where to look for answers when you need them.

MATERIALS AND EQUIPMENT

Yarn

One of the nice things about these small projects is that you can use almost any yarn you have left over from another project in their construction. That being said, I do have suggestions about which yarns may be the easiest to use, thus providing the best results.

I chose four yarns from the Brown Sheep Yarn Company to make the samples in this book. I love Brown Sheep Yarns because they are made in the USA with natural fibers, come in a great palette of colors, and they are from a wonderful family-owned and operated company. I'd like to tell you about the yarns I used before I talk about substitutes.

Brown Sheep Lamb's Pride Worsted

15% mohair, 85% wool
190 yards per skein
98 colors

Brown Sheep Cotton Fleece

80% pima cotton, 20% merino wool
215 yards per skein
60 colors

Brown Sheep Nature Spun Worsted

100% wool
245 yards per skein
80 colors

Brown Sheep Serendipity Tweed

60% pima cotton, 40% wool
210 yards per skein
32 colors (and growing)

In addition to these main yarns, I used several yarns from other companies when I needed qualities not available in the Brown Sheep line-up. I used scraps of Noro Kureyon for the snail shell and the toucan beak; I used Plymouth Select Boucle Merino Superwash as the sheepy yarn in Ewe and Lamb; and I used Baby Kid Extra by Filatura Di Crosa as a carry-along yarn in the goslings and chicks to give them extra fluff, and in the fringe in front of the koala's ears.

Can you use other yarns? Of course you can. You can even use other yarn weights to make small, pocket-sized toys (from sock or lace weight yarns) or larger, sturdier toys (from bulky weight yarns). Success will be dependent on your gauge.

For all of the worsted weight toys in this book, I used a gauge of 20 sts and 24 rows = 4" in stockinet stitch, which I achieved with US size 6 needles. For Cotton Fleece and Serendipity Tweed, I went down two sizes in needles, resulting in a different gauge, but producing a dense fabric suitable for knitted toys. It is extremely important, whatever yarn you are using, to produce a firm, dense fabric. This will give the toy body, make it easier to shape, and ensure that stuffing will not be visible between the stitches. I suggest that you swatch with needles two sizes smaller than those recommended for the yarn you are using. If the result is a smooth, firm, dense fabric, then you've found the right gauge. If you are a loose knitter, you may have to downsize further. Likewise, if you are a tight knitter, you may not need to downsize at all. As with all successful knitting, you will need to make a gauge swatch before you begin, not to match a set of numbers, but to evaluate the characteristics of the fabric you are producing.

I have made hundreds of knitted, stuffed toys over the years. The yarns that are easiest to work with contain non-superwash wool, either exclusively or as part of a blend. The natural scales on the yarn allow it to shape more easily and contribute to easy finishing because, when pulled through the stuffing, the yarn stays in place without knots. You may, of course, use any yarn you like, but you will have a bit more difficulty with the shaping and finishing if the yarn does not contain wool.

The yardage requirements given with each pattern are based on my knitting tension with the stated yarns, plus a little extra just in case. These yardage requirements must be considered approximate, especially if you are using a different yarn and knitting at a different tension.

Stuffing

Next to yarn, the most important element of a knitted toy is the stuffing. You may, of course, use any stuffing you like, including carded wool. I prefer a polyester fiberfill-like stuffing because it will help the toy keep its shape and contribute to washability. Not all fiberfill stuffings are equal, however. Even a product marked "premium" can result in clumping and may not have the resilience for a good, huggable toy.

Years ago, my sister-in-law purchased a new sofa for her living room. She found that the cushions where much too cushy, and removed a lot of the fiberfill stuffing. She gave me several trash bags full for crafting and, when I made my first knitted toys (in 2005), I used this cast-off filling to stuff them. I noticed that the fiberfill was "slippery," that is, the fibers slid past each other and slid through my fingers. This was not a property I noticed in other fiber fillings I had been buying at the fabric store. I also noticed that the stuffing filled the toys evenly, without clumping, no matter how much or little I used, and the toys were extremely resilient when squished, always springing back into perfect form. All too soon I had used up all of this stuffing and had to go in search of more.

In looking for a similar, commercially-available stuffing, I used my fingers to determine the slipperiness of the fibers. Eventually I found a product that produced wonderful results: Soft 'n Crafty, sold by Jo-Ann Fabrics. I've had some difficulty finding this at Jo-Ann stores lately. It is sold under the Jo-Ann label but made by Fairfield. You can read about all the Fairfield stuffing products at http://www.fairfieldworld.com/product-cat/19-polyester-fiberfills, and even order them on-line. It was on this web site that I learned that the slippery property of stuffing that is ideal for toys is due to siliconized polyester fibers.

You can also use dried beans or poly "beads" (available at craft stores) to add weight to the bottoms of your knitted toys to make them sit more easily. As a safety note, should you decide to employ this method, please sew the beans or beads into a muslin bag before placing them inside the toy. Small beans or beads could easily work their way through the knitted fabric and become choking hazards.

Knitting Needles

All the patterns in this book require circular knitting. Instructions are written such that you can use any method of circular knitting you like. Choose the needles based on your circular knitting style: double-pointed, two circular needles, or one long circular (for Magic Loop knitting). You will need to swatch with your yarn choice to determine needle size.

OTHER EQUIPMENT

You will also need a tapestry needle (for finishing and embroidery) and a suitably-sized crochet hook (for attaching fringe). You may find it useful to use a pencil with an intact eraser (for stuffing narrow pieces) and a clean, old toothbrush (for fluffing up mohair yarn in fluffy toys like the chicks and goslings).

GENERAL INSTRUCTIONS

Finishing techniques are essential to the success of these knitted toys. I use the mattress stitch technique for attaching pieces. Done well, this technique will make the attached pieces appear to be integral to the body. Excellent tutorials on joining with mattress stitch can be found on my DVD, *Knitting Fundamentals, A Reference Guide* (available through amazon.com), and on the Internet. Try a *YouTube* search.

The instruction "weave through" or "weave in" used in these patterns means to use the tapestry needle to take the end through the stuffing to the back side of the toy. You can then add a bit of tension and snip off the tail. The friction between the stuffing and the scales on the wool will hold the end in place. In some instances, it is necessary to weave in an end on a piece that does not have stuffing or is not yet stuffed. If the piece is flat, you can weave in as you ordinarily would on any piece of knitting. If the piece was worked in the round and is not yet stuffed, but is a tiny piece like the ball on the end of a leg, you can weave in from the right side by weaving over and under the "bars" between columns of stitches.

When working embroidery stitches, it is likewise not necessary to tie a knot at the beginning or end. Simply bring the wool through the stuffing from the back of the toy to the front and work the embroidery. When finished, take the end through the stuffing to the back, add a bit of tension and snip off the beginning and ending tails.

Small pieces should be attached securely to prevent becoming choking hazards if they come loose. If very small children will have access to the toy, you may use knots to secure stitching when sewing on ears, horns, tails, or other small pieces. Details involving short fringes should not be used on toys for very small children.

WASHING

These knitted toys can be washed as you would wash any fine knitting. Use a wool soak or mild shampoo to soak the toy in a sink with tepid water for 10 to 15 minutes. Then gently rinse and press out the water. Roll the toy in a towel and gently squeeze to remove as much water as possible. Reshape as necessary and allow it to dry thoroughly.

Basic Bottoms

As you scan through the toys in this book, you may notice that a number of them share a similar body type. In fact, the majority of toys in this book start with the same instructions. To save space, which means printing costs, and ultimately lower the price I'll have to charge for the book, I decided not to repeat instructions that are widely shared between the toys. That is the purpose of this section.

Flipping back and forth while knitting is not fun, I know. Feel free to photocopy the basic bottom and bird bottom instructions to travel through the book with you as you knit.

Please note: Unless otherwise stated, all patterns in this book have the beginning of the round positioned at center back.

Basic bottom

CO 6. Join in a round.

Round 1 kfb around: 12 sts

Round 2 knit

Round 3 kfb around: 24 sts

Rounds 4-5 knit

Round 6 *kfb, k1, rep from * around: 36 sts

Rounds 7-9 knit

Round 10 *kfb, k2, rep from * around: 48 sts

Rounds 11-14 knit

Round 15 *kfb, k3, rep from * around: 60 sts

Bird bottom

Work basic bottom (above) through round 11: 48 sts

Shape tail: The tail is shaped working back and forth with short rows.

Row 1 k1, ssk, k1, turn

Row 2 sl1, p3, p2tog, p1, turn

Row 3 sl1, k4, ssk, k1, turn

Row 4 sl1, p5, p2tog, p1, turn

Row 5 sl1, k6, ssk, wrap the next st and turn

Row 6 p7, p2tog, wrap the next st and turn

Row 7 k4 (to center back)

Finish by knitting the next round: k4, knit the next st with its wrap, k32, knit the next st with its wrap, k4.

Forty-two (42) sts remain in the round.

Large bird bottom

Work basic bottom (above) through round 15: 60 sts.

Knit one round.

Shape tail: The tail is shaped working back and forth with short rows.

Row 1 k1, ssk, k1, turn

Row 2 sl1, p3, p2tog, p1, turn

Row 3 sl1, k4, ssk, k1, turn

Row 4 sl1, p5, p2tog, p1, turn

Row 5 sl1, k6, ssk, k1, turn

Row 6 sl1, p7, p2tog, p1, turn

Row 7 sl1, k8, ssk, wrap the next st and turn

Row 8 p9, p2tog, wrap the next st and turn

Row 9 k5 (to center back)

Finish by knitting the next round: k5, knit the next st with its wrap, k40, knit the next st with its wrap, k5.

Fifty-two (52) sts remain in the round.

Notes, Techniques, and Abbreviations

Notes
1. Before you begin, please check our web site (TimelessKnitsPublications.com) for errata (corrections) to the published instructions.

Techniques
1. Garter stitch is produced by knitting every row (when knitting flat), or alternating knit with purl rounds (when knitting in the round).

2. I-cord is worked on two double-pointed needles. Cast on the specified number of stitches. Do not turn work. Slide the stitches to the other end of the needle such that the first stitch you will knit is at the opposite end of the stitches from the working yarn. Knit all the stitches, applying extra tension to the first stitch to pull the yarn across the back. Slide the stitches again, give the cord end a tug, pull the yarn across the back, and knit the next row. Repeat this process until the cord is the desired length.

3. JMCO (Judy's Magic Cast-On): Created by Judy Becker, this marvelous cast on is explained on knitty.com (knitty.com/ISSUEspring06/FEATmagiccaston.html), and demonstrated in many videos on YouTube (http://www.youtube.com/). Or see Judy's book, *Beyond Toes: Knitting Adventures With Judy's Magic Cast-On*. JMCO is especially useful when a piece is to be knit in both directions from the cast-on, as it results in a seamless beginning.

4. Kitchener stitch: With the stitches to be grafted on two parallel, double-pointed needles, make sure that the working yarn is coming from the back needle. To start, take the tapestry needle through the first stitch on the front needle as if to purl and leave the stitch on the needle. Now go through the first stitch on the back needle as if to knit and leave this stitch on the needle. Keep the working yarn below the needles. You will now work two stitches on the front needle followed by two stitches on the back needle, across the row, as follows: On the front needle go through the first stitch as if to knit and drop it off the needle. Go through the second stitch as if to purl and leave it on the needle. Tighten the yarn. On the back needle go through the first stitch as if to purl and drop it off the needle. Go through the second stitch as if to knit and leave it on the needle. Tighten the yarn. When there is only one stitch left on each needle, go through the front stitch as if to knit and drop it off the needle. Go through the back stitch as if to purl and drop it off the needle. Pull the tail to the inside and weave in.

5. **Pick up and knit stitches:** Place the tip of the right-hand needle into an edge stitch or the edge of a stitch; wrap the needle with working yarn (as if knitting); pull the loop through as the "picked up" stitch.

6. **Stockinet stitch** is produced by alternating knit and purl rows (when knitting flat), or knitting every round (when knitting in the round).

7. **Three-needle bind off:** With stitches to be bound off on two needles, use a third needle to knit one stitch through the first stitch on *both* needles. Now repeat, knitting a second stitch through the second stitch on *both* needles. Pull the first stitch knit over the second stitch as for a regular bind off, and continue knitting a stitch from the front needle together with a stitch from the back needle and binding off across the row until all stitches are bound off.

8. **Twisted cord:** Knot the ends of two lengths of yarn together. Each strand should be about 4 times longer than the finished length desired. Holding one knot firmly in one hand, insert your finger into the other end and begin to add twist by twisting your hand. Add enough twist that, when relaxed, the cord begins to double back on itself. Fold the cord at the midpoint and let it twist back on itself. Tie a knot in the unfolded end and trim.

9. **Waste yarn:** A scrap of smooth yarn of a contrasting color.

10. **Wrap a stitch:** In shaping with short rows, it is sometimes necessary to wrap a stitch before turning to prevent a hole in the knitting where the row ended short. On a knit row, knit to the directed point in the row; then, bring the working yarn to the front of the work between the needles. Slip the next stitch (as if to purl) from the left-hand needle to the right-hand needle. Take the working yarn to the back of the work between the needles. Finish by replacing the slipped and wrapped stitch back to the left-hand needle without twisting. On a purl row, purl to the directed point in the row; then, take the working yarn to the back of the work between the needles. Slip the next stitch (as if to purl) from the left-hand needle to the right-hand needle. Bring the working yarn to the front of the work between the needles. Finish by replacing the slipped and wrapped stitch back to the left-hand needle without twisting. The wraps sometimes get worked together with their corresponding stitches when the short rows are completed.

Abbreviations

BO: Bind off

cdd: Centered double decrease—Slip next 2 sts as if to knit, k1, p2sso

CO: Cast on

k: Knit

k2tog: Knit 2 sts together—a right-slanting decrease

kfb: Knit in the front and the back of the same st—an increase

M1L (make one—left slanting): Bring the tip of the left-hand needle under the strand between needles, from front to back. Knit through the back of the loop.

M1R (make one—right slanting): Bring the tip of the left-hand needle under the strand between needles, from back to front. Knit this loop.

MB (make bobble): *knit in the front/the back/the front/the back/and the front again of the next st, pull the first 4 loops from this group over the 5th loop.

psso: pass slipped st over the st just worked

p2sso: pass 2 slipped sts over the st just worked

p: Purl

p2tog: Purl two sts together—a right-slanting decrease

pfb: Purl in the front and back of the st—an increase

rep: Repeat

RS: Right side

sl[x]: Slip the next st or sts (without twisting)

ssk (slip, slip, knit—a left-slanting decrease): Slip two sts individually from left to right needle, as if to knit. Place tip of left needle through front loops of both slipped sts and knit them together.

st / sts: Stitch / stitches

tbl/tbls: Through the back loop(s)

WS: Wrong side

EMBROIDERY STITCHES

Embroidery stitches provide important detail and impart personality to these hand-knit toys. The stitches I used are all fairly basic; each is illustrated below.

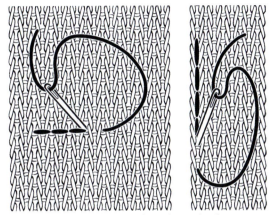
Back stitch, horizontal and vertical

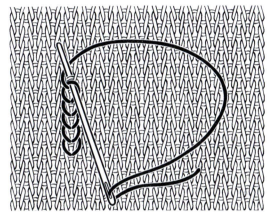
Chain stitch

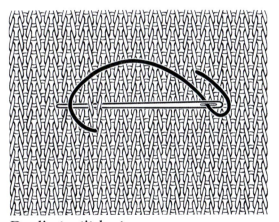
Duplicate stitch, step one

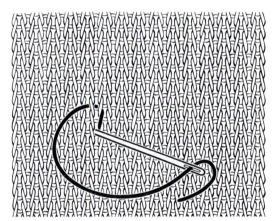
Duplicate stitch, step two

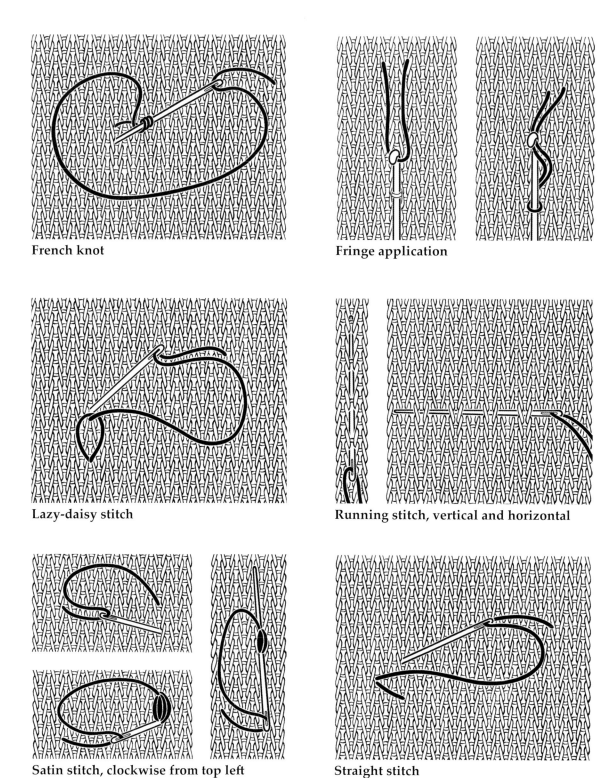

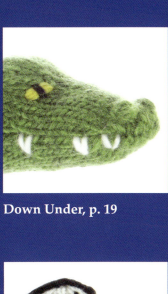 Down Under, p. 19

 Flock, p. 35

 Heartland, p. 51

 Midnight Sun, p. 73

 Reef, p. 87

 Serengeti, p. 103

 Southwest, p. 119

 Wetlands, p. 133

 Woodlands, p. 147

Down Under

I can think of few other places that have such unusual wildlife. All children seem to love kangaroos — how special that our kangaroo also has a removable joey. And we've included a kiwi because, after all, New Zealand is also Down Under.

Crocodile

YARN
Brown Sheep Lamb's Pride Worsted colors M191 (Kiwi), M11 (White Frost), M155 (Lemon Drop), and M05 (Onyx)

YARDAGE
Green, 50 yds
White, yellow, and black, 1 yd each

MEASUREMENTS
Crocodile is 13-1/2" long.

NOTES
1. Please read the Read Me First chapter, pp. 6-16 before you begin.

INSTRUCTIONS

TAIL (worked in the round)

Beginning at the tip of the tail, CO 6. Join in a round.

Rounds 1-10 knit
Round 11 *kfb, k1, rep from * around: 9 sts
Rounds 12-21 knit
Round 22 *kfb, k2, rep from * around: 12 sts
Rounds 23-32 knit
Round 33 *kfb, k3, rep from * around: 15 sts
Rounds 34-43 knit
Round 44 *kfb, k4, rep from * around: 18 sts

Leaving sts on the needle(s), lightly stuff tail.

Rounds 45-54 knit
Round 55 *kfb, k5, rep from * around: 21 sts
Rounds 56-60 knit
Round 61 *kfb, k6, rep from * around: 24 sts
Rounds 62-66 knit
Round 67 *kfb, k7, rep from * around: 27 sts
Rounds 68-72 knit
Round 73 *kfb, k8, rep from * around: 30 sts

Leaving sts on the needle(s), lightly stuff tail.

BODY (continue working in the round)

Rounds 1-15 knit
Round 16 *k2, ssk, k2, k2tog, k2, rep from * around: 24 sts
Rounds 17-18 knit

Leaving sts on the needle(s), lightly stuff body.

End by knitting 6 sts; round now begins at the left side of the jaw.

HEAD (continue working in the round)

Round 1 [kfb] twice, k8, [kfb] 4 times, k8, [kfb] twice: 32 sts
Round 2 knit
Round 3 k20, [kfb] 8 times, k4: 40 sts
Round 4 k2tog, k12, ssk, k2tog, k20, ssk: 36 sts
Round 5 knit
Round 6 k2tog, k10, ssk, k2tog, k18, ssk: 32 sts
Round 7 k16, ssk, k2, ssk, k2tog, k2, k2tog, k4: 28 sts
Round 8 k2tog, k8, ssk, k2tog, k12, k2tog: 24 sts
Round 9 k13, [ssk] twice, [k2tog] twice, k3: 20 sts
Rounds 10-19 knit

Leaving sts on the needle(s), lightly stuff head.

Round 20 *k2tog, k6, ssk, rep from *: 16 sts
Round 21 knit
Round 22 k2tog, k4, ssk, k2tog, MB, k2, MB, ssk: 12 sts
Round 23 knit
Round 24 *k2tog, k2, ssk, rep from *: 8 sts

Leaving sts on the needle(s), lightly stuff mouth and snout.

With 4 sts above (upper jaw) and 4 sts below (lower jaw) use the Kitchener stitch to graft snout.

Legs and feet (make 4)

Beginning with foot, CO 13.

Row 1 k5, cdd, k5: 11 sts
Row 2 k5, p1, k5
Row 3 k4, cdd, k4: 9 sts
Row 4 k4, p1, k4
Row 5 k3, cdd, k3: 7 sts
Row 6 k3, p1, k3
Join in a round.

Round 1 k3, k2tog, k2: 6 sts
Rounds 2-20 knit
BO. Repeat for other three legs.

Assembly and finishing

Sew legs to body as shown. With white, using straight stitches, make teeth as shown on either side of mouth and snout. With yellow, use satin stitch to make an eye on either side of head as shown. With black, make a straight-stitch pupil over each eye as shown.

Kangaroo & Joey

YARN
Brown Sheep Lamb's Pride Worsted colors M174 (Wild Mustard) and M02 (Brown Heather)

YARDAGE
Gold: Kangaroo, 120 yds; Joey, 24 yds
Brown: Kangaroo, 1 yd; Joey, 1 yd

MEASUREMENTS
Kangaroo is 7-1/2" tall; Joey is 3" tall.

NOTES
1. Please read the Read Me First chapter, pp. 6-16 before you begin.

KANGAROO

INSTRUCTIONS
Work basic bottom, p. 11, through round 15: 60 sts.

BODY (continue working in the round)

Rounds 1-6 knit
Round 7 *k2, ssk, k12, k2tog, k2, rep from * around: 54 sts
Rounds 8-15 knit
Round 16 *k2, ssk, k10, k2tog, k2, rep from * around: 48 sts
Rounds 17-22 knit
Round 23 *k2, ssk, k8, k2tog, k2, rep from * around: 42 sts
Rounds 24-27 knit
Round 28 *k2, ssk, k6, k2tog, k2, rep from * around: 36 sts
Rounds 29-32 knit
Round 33 *k2, ssk, k4, k2tog, k2, rep from * around: 30 sts
Rounds 34-35 knit
Round 36 *k2, ssk, k2, k2tog, k2, rep from * around: 24 sts
Round 37 knit

Leaving sts on the needle(s), stuff body.

Round 38 k6, [k2tog] 6 times, k6: 18 sts
Round 39 knit

BACK NECK (worked flat over 12 sts at center back; round begins at center of these sts)

Knit the first 6 sts of the next round. Turn.

Row 1 sl1, p11
Row 2 sl1, k11

Repeat rows 1 and 2 a total of 6 times (12 rows total).

SHAPE CROWN (short rows)

Row 1 sl1, p6, p2tog, p1, turn
Row 2 sl1, k3, ssk, k1, turn
Row 3 sl1, p4, p2tog, p1, turn
Row 4 sl1, k5, ssk, k1, turn
Row 5 sl1, p5, p2tog, turn
Row 6 sl1, k4, ssk

Six (6) sts remain in crown.

From the RS, pick up and knit 8 sts along the left side of neck; k1, ssk, k2tog, k1 at center front neck; pick up and knit 8 sts along the right side of neck; k3 sts from crown. Round (26 sts) now begins at center crown.

FACE (worked in the round)

Round 1 k8, [kfb] 3 times, ssk, k2tog, [kfb] 3 times, k8: 30 sts
Round 2 knit
Round 3 k1, ssk, k3, k2tog, k14, ssk, k3, k2tog, k1: 26 sts
Round 4 knit
Round 5 k1, ssk, k3, k2tog, k2, ssk, k2, k2tog, k2, ssk, k3, k2tog, k1: 20 sts
Round 6 knit
Round 7 k7, ssk, k2, k2tog, k7: 18 sts
Round 8 knit
Round 9 k6, ssk, k2, k2tog, k6: 16 sts
Round 10 knit
Round 11 k1, [ssk] 3 times, k2, [k2tog] 3 times, k1: 10 sts
Rounds 12-14 knit

Leaving sts on the needle(s), stuff neck, head, and face.

Round 15 [ssk] 2 times, k2, [k2tog] 2 times: 6 sts

Leaving sts on the needle(s), stuff nose. Break yarn, thread tail through remaining sts, pull up and weave through.

EARS (worked flat, make 2)

CO 5.

Row 1 purl
Row 2 k1, kfb, k1, kfb, k1: 7 sts
Row 3 purl
Row 4 knit
Row 5 purl
Row 6 knit
Row 7 purl
Row 8 k1, ssk, k1, k2tog, k1: 5 sts
Row 9 purl
Row 10 knit
Row 11 purl
Row 12 ssk, k1, k2tog: 3 sts
Row 13 purl
Row 14 sl2 sts together as if to knit, k1, p2sso: 1 st

BO. Repeat for second ear.

TAIL (worked in the round)

CO 27. Join in a round.

Round 1 k12, cdd, k12: 25 sts
Round 2 knit
Round 3 k11, cdd, k11: 23 sts
Round 4 knit

Round 5 k10, cdd, k10: 21 sts
Round 6 knit
Round 7 k9, cdd, k9: 19 sts
Round 8 k2tog, k17: 18 sts
Round 9 k14, wrap the next st and turn; p10, wrap the next st and turn; k10, knit the wrap with the next st, k3
Round 10 k3, knit the wrap with the next st, k14
Round 11 knit
Rounds 12-14 rep rounds 9-11
Rounds 15-17 rep rounds 9-11
Round 18 *k2, k2tog, k2, rep from * around: 15 sts
Rounds 19-30 knit
Round 31 *k1, k2tog, k2, rep from * around: 12 sts
Rounds 32-41 knit
Round 42 *k1, k2tog, k1, rep from * around: 9 sts
Rounds 43-50 knit
Round 51 *k2tog, k1, rep from * around: 6 sts
Rounds 52-57 knit
Round 58 k2tog around: 3 sts

Break yarn, thread tail through remaining sts, pull up and weave through. Stuff tail.

FEET (worked in the round, make 2)

CO 9. Join in a round.

Rounds 1-18 knit

Break yarn, thread tail through remaining sts, pull up and weave through.

Stuff front half, leaving back half (toward CO edge) unstuffed. Repeat for second foot.

FRONT LEGS AND PAWS (worked in the round, make 2)

CO 6. Join in a round.

Rounds 1-18 knit

Break yarn, thread tail through remaining sts, pull up and weave through.

Stuff paws only (about 1/3 of the length). Repeat for second leg and paw.

POUCH (worked flat)

CO 8.

Row 1 purl
Row 2 CO 2; [kfb] 10 times: 20 sts
Row 3 CO 2; [pfb] 2 times, p to end: 24 sts
Rows 4, 6, 8, 10, 12, 14, 16, 18 knit
Rows 5, 7, 9, 11, 13, 15, 17 purl
Row 19 p2tog, *k1, p1, rep from * across: 23 sts
Row 20 k1, *p1, k1, rep from * across
Row 21 p1, *k1, p1, rep from * across
Row 22 rep row 20
Row 23 rep row 21

BO in established ribbing pattern.

Timeless Toys   25

Assembly and finishing Sew ears in place on either side of crown. With brown, make satin stitch eyes and a satin stitch nose as shown. Sew pouch, tail, feet, and front legs and paws to body as shown.

Joey Instructions

Work basic bottom, p. 11, through round 3: 24 sts.

Body (continue working in the round)

Rounds 1-4 knit
Round 5 *k1, ssk, k2, k2tog, k1, rep from * around: 18 sts
Rounds 6-9 knit
Round 10 *k1, ssk, k2tog, k1, rep from * around: 12 sts
Round 11 knit

Leaving sts on the needle(s), stuff body.

Round 12 k2tog around: 6 sts

BACK NECK (worked flat over 4 sts at center back; round begins at center of these sts)

Knit the first 2 sts of the next round. Turn.

Row 1 sl1, p3
Row 2 sl1, k3

Repeat rows 1 and 2 a total of 4 times (8 rows total).

Pick up and knit 4 sts along left side of neck; k2 sts at center front; pick up and knit 4 sts along right side of neck; k2 sts from back neck. Round (14 sts) now begins at center back.

FACE (worked in the round)

Round 1 knit
Round 2 ssk, k2, k2tog, k2, ssk, k2, k2tog: 10 sts
Round 3 knit

Leaving sts on the needle(s), stuff neck and head.

Round 4 ssk, k6, k2tog: 8 sts

Leaving sts on the needle(s), stuff neck, head, and face.

Round 5 knit
Rounds 6 ssk, k4, k2tog: 6 sts

Leaving sts on the needle(s), stuff nose. Break yarn, thread tail through remaining sts, pull up and weave through.

EARS (worked flat, make 2)

CO 3.

Row 1 purl
Row 2 knit
Row 3 purl
Row 4 sl2 sts together as if to knit, k1, p2sso: 1 st

BO. Repeat for second ear.

TAIL (worked in the round)

CO 13. Join in a round.

Round 1 k5, cdd, k5: 11 sts
Round 2 knit
Round 3 k4, cdd, k4: 9 sts
Round 4 knit
Round 5 k3, cdd, k3: 7 sts
Round 6 k2tog, k5: 6 sts
Rounds 7-12 knit
Round 13 [k2tog] 3 times onto one needle: 3 sts

Work 6 rows of 3-st I-cord. BO.

FEET (make 2)

CO 3.

Work 4 rows of 3-st I-cord. BO.

Repeat for second foot.

ASSEMBLY AND FINISHING

Sew ears in place on either side of crown. With brown, make satin stitch eyes and a satin stitch nose as shown. Sew tail and feet to body as shown.

Kiwi

YARN
Brown Sheep Lamb's Pride Worsted colors M02 (Brown Heather), M155 (Lemon Drop), and M05 (Onyx)

YARDAGE
Brown, 110 yds
Yellow, 15 yds
Black, 1/2 yd

MEASUREMENTS
Kiwi is 8" tall.

NOTES
1. Please read the Read Me First chapter, pp. 6-16 before you begin.

INSTRUCTIONS
With brown, work basic bottom, p. 11, through round 15: 60 sts.

BODY (continue working in the round)

Rounds 1-10 knit
Round 11 *k2, ssk, k12, k2tog, k2, rep from * around: 54 sts
Rounds 12-14 knit
Round 15 *k2, ssk, k10, k2tog, k2, rep from * around: 48 sts
Rounds 16-18 knit
Round 19 *k2, ssk, k8, k2tog, k2, rep from * around: 42 sts
Rounds 20-22 knit
Round 23 *k2, ssk, k6, k2tog, k2, rep from * around: 36 sts
Rounds 24-26 knit
Round 27 *k2, ssk, k4, k2tog, k2, rep from * around: 30 sts
Rounds 28-30 knit
Round 31 *k2, ssk, k2, k2tog, k2, rep from * around: 24 sts

Leaving sts on the needle(s), lightly stuff body.

Round 32 knit
Round 33 *k2, ssk, k2tog, k2, rep from * around: 18 sts
Rounds 34-39 knit

Head (continue working in the round)

Round 1 *k2, [kfb] twice, k2, rep from * around: 24 sts
Round 2 k6, wrap the next st and turn; p12, wrap the next st and turn; p6
Round 3 k6, knit the wrap with the next st, k10, knit the wrap with the next st tbls, k6
Rounds 4-11 Rep rounds 2 and 3 four times more
Round 12 *k2, ssk, k2tog, k2, rep from * around: 18 sts
Round 13 knit

Leaving sts on the needle(s), lightly stuff neck and head.

Round 14 k2tog around: 9 sts
Round 15 knit
Round 16 k2tog, k5, ssk: 7 sts

Break yarn, thread tail through remaining sts, pull up and weave through.

Beak (worked in the round)

With yellow, CO 9. Join in a round.

Rounds 1-2 knit
Round 3 *k2tog, k1, rep from * around: 6 sts
Rounds 4-6 knit
Round 7 k2tog around onto one needle: 3 sts

Work in 3-st I-cord for 18 rows. BO.

Feet (make 2)

With yellow, make six 3-st I-cord toes, as follows:

CO 3. Work in I-cord for 7 rows. BO.

Sew toes together in groups of three at one end as shown.

Legs (worked in the round, make 2)

With yellow, CO 6. Join in a round.

Rounds 1-12 knit
Switch to brown.
Round 13 kfb around: 12 sts
Rounds 14-22 knit

BO. Repeat for second leg.

Assembly and finishing

Sew beak to face as shown. Sew legs to back of feet as shown; sew legs to front of body as shown. With black, make two French knot eyes.

Timeless Toys   29

Koala

Yarn
Brown Sheep Lamb's Pride Worsted colors M03 (Grey Heather), M05 (Onyx), and M89 (Roasted Coffee)

Yardage
Grey, 60 yds
Black, 2 yds
Brown, 1 yd

Measurements
Koala is 6" tall.

Notes
1. Please read the Read Me First chapter, pp. 6-16 before you begin.

Instructions
With grey, work basic bottom, p. 11, through round 10: 48 sts.

Body (continue working in the round)

Rounds 1-20 knit
Round 21 *k2tog, k2, rep from * around: 36 sts
Rounds 22-24 knit
Round 25 *k2tog, k1, rep from * around: 24 sts
Rounds 26-27 knit
Round 28 k6, [k2tog] 6 times, k6: 18 sts

Leaving sts on the needle(s), stuff body.

Back neck (worked flat over 12 sts at center back)

Row 1 k6, turn
Row 2 sl1, p11
Row 3 sl1, k11

Rep rows 2 and 3 a total of six times (12 rows).

Shape crown (short rows)

Row 1 p7, p2tog, p1, turn
Row 2 sl1, k3, ssk, k1, turn
Row 3 sl1, p4, p2tog, p1, turn
Row 4 sl1, k5, ssk, turn
Row 5 sl1, p5, p2tog, turn
Row 6 sl1, k4, ssk

Six (6) sts remain in crown.

Pick up and knit 7 sts along the left side of back neck; k2, [kfb] twice, k2 (at center front); pick up and knit 7 sts along the right side of back neck; k3 from crown. Round (28 sts) now begins at center crown.

Face (worked in the round)

Round 1 k13, [kfb] twice, k13: 30 sts
Round 2 k1, ssk, k24, k2tog, k1: 28 sts
Round 3 knit
Round 4 k1, ssk, k22, k2tog, k1: 26 sts
Round 5 knit
Round 6 k1, ssk, k20, k2tog, k1: 24 sts
Rounds 7-8 knit

Leaving sts on the needle(s), lightly stuff neck and face.

Round 9 k2tog around: 12 sts
Round 10 knit
Round 11 k2tog around: 6 sts

Add stuffing to round out face. Break yarn, thread tail through remaining sts, pull up and weave through.

Nose (worked flat)

With black, CO 3.

Row 1 purl
Row 2 kfb across: 6 sts
Row 3 purl
Row 4 k2, k2tog, k2: 5 sts
Row 5 purl
Row 6 ssk, k1, k2tog: 3 sts
Row 7 purl
Row 8 sl2 as if to knit, k1, p2sso: 1 st

Ears (worked flat, make 2)

CO 7.

Row 1 pfb, p4, pfb, p1: 9 sts
Row 2 knit
Row 3 pfb, p6, pfb, p1: 11 sts
Row 4 knit
Row 5 purl
Row 6 knit
Row 7 purl
Row 8 ssk, k7, k2tog: 9 sts
Row 9 purl
Row 10 ssk, k5, k2tog: 7 sts
Row 11 purl

BO, working an ssk in the first 2 sts and a k2tog in the last 2 sts. Repeat for second ear.

Legs and feet (worked in the round, make 4)

CO 9. Join in a round.

Rounds 1-12 knit
Round 13 k2, [kfb] 5 times, k2: 14 sts
Rounds 14-17 knit
Round 18 k2, [k2tog] 5 times, k2: 9 sts
Round 20 *k2tog, k1, rep from * around: 6 sts

Break yarn, thread tail through remaining sts, pull up and weave through. Stuff just the foot, leaving leg unstuffed. Repeat for other three legs.

Assembly and finishing

Sew nose to face as shown, adding a bit of stuffing behind. Sew ears to crown, wrong side facing front. Cut four or five fringes per ear and attach in front of ear as shown. With brown, make satin stitch eyes. Sew legs and feet to front as shown.

Platypus

YARN
Brown Sheep Lamb's Pride Worsted colors M175 (Bronze Patina) and M05 (Onyx)

YARDAGE
Brown, 95 yds
Black, 15 yds

MEASUREMENTS
Platypus is 14" long.

NOTES
1. Please read the Read Me First chapter, pp. 6-16 before you begin.

INSTRUCTIONS
With brown, work basic bottom, p. 11, through round 10: 48 sts.

BODY (continue working in the round)

Rounds 1-30 knit
Round 31 *k2tog, k2, rep from * around: 36 sts
Rounds 32-34 knit
Round 35 *k2tog, k1, rep from * around: 24 sts
Rounds 36-37 knit

Leaving sts on the needle(s), very slightly stuff body, squishing so that body is wider from side to side than from front to back.

Round 38 *k2tog around: 12 sts

HEAD (continue working in the round)

Round 1 knit
Round 2 kfb around: 24 sts
Round 3 knit
Round 4 *kfb, k1, rep from * around: 36 sts
Round 5 knit
Round 6 k9, wrap the next st and turn; p18, wrap the next st and turn; k9
Round 7 k9, knit the wrap with the next st, k16, knit the wrap with the next st, k9
Rounds 8-11 Rep rounds 6 and 7 twice more
Round 12 [ssk] twice, k4, k2tog, k4, ssk, k4, k2tog, k4, ssk, k4, [k2tog] twice: 28 sts
Round 13 knit
Round 14 ssk, k24, k2tog: 26 sts

Round 15 knit
Round 16 ssk, k22, k2tog: 24 sts
Round 17 knit

Leaving sts on the needle(s), lightly stuff neck and head.

Round 18 k2tog around: 12 sts
Round 19 knit

K3. Redistribute sts so there are six sts on the top and six sts on the bottom. Join with a three-needle bind off, adding stuffing if needed.

DUCKBILL (worked in the round)

With black, use JMCO (see Technique 3, p. 12) to CO 6.

Round 1 *[kfb] twice, k1, rep from *: 10 sts
Round 2 knit
Round 3 *kfb, k2, kfb, k1, rep from *: 14 sts
Round 4 knit
Round 5 *kfb, k4, kfb, k1, rep from *: 18 sts
Rounds 6-15 knit
Round 16 *[kfb] twice, k5, [kfb] twice, rep from *: 26 sts
Round 17 knit
Round 18 k10, wrap the next st and turn; p7, wrap the next st and turn; p5, wrap the next st and turn; k5, knit the wraps with the next 2 sts, k15

BO. Gently stuff the front of the bill.

TAIL (worked in the round)

With brown, use JMCO to CO 18.

Round 1 *kfb, k6, kfb, k1, rep from *: 22 sts
Round 2 knit
Round 3 *kfb, k8, kfb, k1, rep from *: 26 sts
Round 4 knit
Round 5 *kfb, k10, kfb, k1, rep from *: 30 sts
Rounds 6-9 knit
Round 10 *ssk, k11, k2tog, rep from *: 26 sts
Rounds 11-15 knit
Round 16 *ssk, k9, k2tog, rep from *: 22 sts
Rounds 17-22 knit
Round 23 *ssk, k7, k2tog, rep from *: 18 sts
Rounds 24-35 knit

BO. Stuff lightly.

FEET AND LEGS (worked in the round, make 4)

Use JMCO to CO 8 (beginning at end of foot).

Round 1 *kfb, k1, rep from * around: 12 sts
Round 2 knit
Round 3 *kfb, k3, kfb, k1, rep from *: 16 sts
Rounds 4-9 knit

Leaving sts on the needle(s), lightly stuff foot.

Round 10 *ssk, k4, k2tog, rep from *: 12 sts
Rounds 11-22 knit

BO. Repeat for the other three feet and legs.

ASSEMBLY AND FINISHING

Sew duckbill to face as shown. Sew legs to body as shown. With black, make French knot eyes and use straight stitches to indicate "webbed" feet. With brown, use duplicate stitches to make nostrils on end of bill as shown.

Flock

Mother Nature really shows her sense of humor when it comes to birds. I've included some of the most colorful and outlandish representatives in my "flock."

Blue-footed Booby

Yarn

Brown Sheep Lamb's Pride Worsted colors M10 (Creme), M02 (Brown Heather), and M187 (Turquoise Depths)

Brown Sheep Serendipity Tweed-color ST84 (Nebraska Wheat) for head

Yardage

Cream, 40 yds
Marled, 5 yds
Brown, 30 yds
Turquoise, 10 yds

Measurements

Blue-footed Booby is 5-3/4" tall, seated.

Notes

1. Please read the Read Me First chapter, pp. 6-16 before you begin.

Instructions

With cream, work bird bottom, p. 11: 42 sts.

Body (continue working in the round)

Rounds 1-6 knit
Round 7 k9, k2tog, k4, ssk, k8, k2tog, k4, ssk, k9: 38 sts
Rounds 8-11 knit
Round 12 k8, k2tog, k4, ssk, k6, k2tog, k4, ssk, k8: 34 sts
Rounds 13-16 knit
Round 17 k7, k2tog, k4, ssk, k4, k2tog, k4, ssk, k7: 30 sts
Rounds 18-20 knit
Round 21 *k2, ssk, k2, k2tog, k2, rep from * around: 24 sts
Round 22 [k2tog] 4 times, ssk, k4, k2tog, [ssk] 4 times: 14 sts

Leaving sts on the needle(s), lightly stuff body.

Head

k4, turn (Back neck is worked flat, beginning with 8 sts at center back)

Switch to marled yarn.

Row 1 sl1, pfb, *p1, pfb, rep from * 2 times more: 12 sts
Row 2 sl1, k11
Row 3 sl1, p11

Rep rows 2 and 3 three times more, then rep row 2 once more.

SHAPE CROWN (short rows)

Row 1 sl1, p6, p2tog, p1, turn
Row 2 sl1, k3, ssk, k1, turn
Row 3 sl1, p4, p2tog, p1, turn
Row 4 sl1, k5, ssk, k1

Eight (8) sts remain in crown.

From the RS, pick up and knit 5 sts along left side of neck; k across 6 sts at center front; pick up and knit 5 sts along right side of neck; k4 from crown. Round (24 sts) now begins at center of crown.

FACE (resume working in the round)

Round 1 knit
Round 2 ssk, k5, k2tog, k6, ssk, k5, k2tog: 20 sts
Round 3 knit
Round 4 ssk, k3, k2tog, ssk, k2, k2tog, ssk, k3, k2tog: 14 sts
Round 5 knit
Round 6 ssk, k10, k2tog: 12 sts

Leaving sts on the needle(s), lightly stuff head.

Round 7 k2tog around: 6 sts

Break yarn, thread tail through remaining sts, pull up and weave through.

BEAK (worked separately, in the round)

With brown, CO 9. Join in a round.

Rounds 1-3 knit
Round 4 *k2tog, k1, rep from * around: 6 sts
Round 5 knit
Round 6 k2tog around: 3 sts

Continue in 3-st I-cord, working for 2 rows.

On the 3rd row, k2tog, k1, BO.

Lightly stuff beak.

WINGS (worked flat, make 2)

With brown, CO 10.

Row 1 [kfb] 7 times, k3: 17 sts
Row 2 knit
Row 3 k14, wrap the next st and turn, knit back

Rep row 3, decreasing the number of sts knit before wrapping and turning by 1 st each time, until only 1 st is knit before wrap and turn.

After wrapping, turning, and knitting back 1, on the next row, k2tog and BO in knit. Repeat for second wing.

FEET AND LEGS (worked flat, make 2)

With turquoise, beginning with foot, CO 17 sts.

Row 1 k8, p1, k8
Row 2 k7, cdd, k7: 15 sts
Row 3 k7, p1, k7
Row 4 k6, cdd, k6: 13 sts
Row 5 k6, p1, k6
Row 6 k5, cdd, k5: 11 sts
Row 7 k5, p1, k5
Row 8 k4, cdd, k4: 9 sts
Row 9 k4, p1, k4
Row 10 k3, cdd, k3: 7 sts
Row 11 k3, p1, k3
Row 12 k2, cdd, k2: 5 sts
Row 13 k2, p1, k2
Row 14 k1, cdd, k1: 3 sts

Do not turn. Row 15 is worked as I-cord.

Row 15 k1, kfb, k1: 4 sts

Continue in 4-st I-cord until leg is 1-3/4" above foot. BO. Repeat for second foot and leg.

ASSEMBLY AND FINISHING

Sew legs to body on either side of front bottom as shown. Sew beak to face as shown. With brown, make 2 French knot eyes. Attach wings as shown.

Flamingo

Yarn
Brown Sheep Lamb's Pride Worsted colors M105 (RPM Pink) and M05 (Onyx)

Yardage
Pink, 70 yds
Black, 5 yds

Measurements
Flamingo is 13" tall (with legs extended).

Notes
1. Please read the Read Me First chapter, pp. 6-16 before you begin.

Instructions
With pink, work bird bottom, p. 11: 42 sts.

Body (continue working in the round)

Rounds 1-6 knit
Round 7 k9, k2tog, k4, ssk, k8, k2tog, k4, ssk, k9: 38 sts
Rounds 8-11 knit
Round 12 k8, k2tog, k4, ssk, k6, k2tog, k4, ssk, k8: 34 sts
Rounds 13-16 knit
Round 17 k7, k2tog, k4, ssk, k4, k2tog, k4, ssk, k7: 30 sts

Rounds 18-20 knit
Round 21 *k2, ssk, k2, k2tog, k2, rep from * around: 24 sts
Round 22 k6, [k2tog] 6 times, k6: 18 sts
Round 23 *k1, ssk, k2tog, k1, rep from * around: 12 sts

Leaving sts on the needle(s), lightly stuff body.

NECK (continue working in the round)

Round 1 knit
Round 2 k8, wrap the next st and turn, p4, wrap the next st and turn, k5, knitting in the wrap with the last st, wrap the next st and turn, p6, purling in the wrap with the last st, wrap the next st and turn, k7, knitting in the wrap with the last st, wrap the next st and turn, p8, purling in the wrap with the last st, wrap the next st and turn, k10, knitting in the wrap with the 9th st
Round 3 rep round 2
Rounds 4-11 knit

Leaving sts on the needle(s), firmly stuff lower neck.

Round 12 rep round 2
Round 13 knit
Round 14 k1, wrap the next st and turn, p2, wrap the next st and turn, k3, knitting in the wrap with the last st, wrap the next st and turn, p4, purling in the wrap with the last st, wrap the next st and turn, k5, knitting in the wrap with the last st, wrap the next st and turn, p6, purling in the wrap with the last st, wrap the next st and turn, k7, knitting in the wrap with the last st, wrap the next st and turn, p8, purling in the wrap with the last st, wrap the next st and turn, knit to the end of the round
Round 15 knit, knitting in wraps with their corresponding sts
Round 16 rep round 14
Round 17 rep round 15
Round 18 rep round 14
Round 19 rep round 15

Leaving sts on the needle(s), firmly stuff upper neck.

HEAD (continue working in the round)

Rounds 1-3 knit
Round 4 ssk, k3, k2tog, k3, k2tog: 9 sts

Leaving sts on the needle(s), stuff head.

BEAK (switch to black)

Rounds 1-3 knit

Leaving sts on the needle(s), stuff beak.

Round 4 *k2tog, k1, rep from * around: 6 sts
Round 5 knit
Round 6 k2tog around: 3 sts

Continue in 3-st I-cord for 2 rows. Last row: k2tog, k1, BO.

FEET AND LEGS (worked flat, make 2)

Beginning with foot, CO 17.

Row 1 k8, p1, k8
Row 2 k7, cdd, k7: 15 sts
Row 3 k7, p1, k7
Row 4 k6, cdd, k6: 13 sts
Row 5 k6, p1, k6
Row 6 k5, cdd, k5: 11 sts
Row 7 k5, p1, k5
Row 8 k4, cdd, k4: 9 sts
Row 9 k4, p1, k4
Row 10 k3, cdd, k3: 7 sts
Row 11 k3, p1, k3
Row 12 k2, cdd, k2: 5 sts
Row 13 k2, p1, k2
Row 14 k1, cdd, k1: 3 sts

Do not turn. Row 15 is worked as I-cord.

Row 15 k1, kfb, k1: 4 sts

Continue in 4-st I-cord until leg is 8″ above foot. BO. Tie a simple knot (for knee joint) at the center of the leg. Repeat for second foot and leg.

ASSEMBLY AND FINISHING

Sew legs to body on either side of front. Cut six 2-1/4″ lengths of pink and attach as for fringe at tail (making tail feathers as shown). Trim tail feathers to 3/4″. With black, make two French knot eyes as shown.

Timeless Toys

Peacock

YARN

Brown Sheep Lamb's Pride Worsted colors M124 (Persian Peacock), M180 (Ruby Red), M22 (Autumn Harvest), M174 (Wild Mustard), M120 (Limeade), and M161 (Violet Fields)

YARDAGE

Blue, 60 yds
Red, orange, yellow, green, blue, and violet (for tail feathers), 5 yds each
Yellow (for toes), 2 yds

MEASUREMENTS

Peacock is 6-1/2" tall.

NOTES

1. Please read the Read Me First chapter, pp. 6-16 before you begin.

INSTRUCTIONS

With blue, work bird bottom, p. 11: 42 sts.

BODY (continue working in the round)

Rounds 1-6 knit
Round 7 k9, k2tog, k4, ssk, k8, k2tog, k4, ssk, k9: 38 sts
Rounds 8-11 knit
Round 12 k8, k2tog, k4, ssk, k6, k2tog, k4, ssk, k8: 34 sts
Rounds 13-16 knit
Round 17 k7, k2tog, k4, ssk, k4, k2tog, k4, ssk, k7: 30 sts
Rounds 18-20 knit
Round 21 *k2, ssk, k2, k2tog, k2, rep from * around: 24 sts
Round 22 [k2tog] 4 times, ssk, k4, k2tog, [ssk] 4 times: 14 sts

Leaving sts on the needle(s), lightly stuff body.

Round 23 k5, ssk, k2tog, k5: 12 sts

NECK (continue working in the round)

Round 1 knit

Round 2 k8, wrap the next st and turn, p4, wrap the next st and turn, k5, knitting in the wrap with the last st, wrap the next st and turn, p6, purling in the wrap with the last st, wrap the next st and turn, k7, knitting in the wrap with the last st, wrap the next st and turn, p8, purling in the wrap with the last st, wrap the next st and turn, k11, knitting in the wrap with the 10th st

Round 3   rep round 2

Rounds 4-7   knit

Leaving sts on the needle(s), firmly stuff lower neck.

Round 8 k1, wrap the next st and turn, p2, wrap the next st and turn, k3, knitting in the wrap with the last st, wrap the next st and turn, p4, purling in the wrap with the last st, wrap the next st and turn, k5, knitting in the wrap with the last st, wrap the next st and turn, p6, purling in the wrap with the last st, wrap the next st and turn, k7, knitting in the wrap with the last st, wrap the next st and turn, p8, purling in the wrap with the last st, wrap the next st and turn, knit to the end of the round

Round 9 k4, knit the next st with its wrap, k2, knit the next st with its wrap, k4

Round 10 k1, wrap the next st and turn, p2, wrap the next st and turn, k3, knitting in the wrap with the last st, wrap the next st and turn, p4, purling in the wrap with the last st, wrap the next st and turn, k5, knitting in the wrap with the last st, wrap the next st and turn, p6, purling in the wrap with the last st, wrap the next st and turn, knit to the end of the round

Round 11 k3, knit the next st with its wrap, k4, knit the next st with its wrap, k3

Leaving sts on the needle(s), firmly stuff upper neck.

Timeless Toys   43

HEAD (continue working in the round)

Round 1 ssk, k3, k2tog, k3, k2tog: 9 sts

BEAK (worked in black; continue working in the round)

Rounds 1-2 knit
Round 3 *k2tog, k1, rep from * around: 6 sts
Round 4 knit

Leaving sts on the needle(s), lightly stuff head and beak.

Round 5 k2tog around: 3 sts

Continue in 3-st I-cord, working for 2 rows. Last row: k2tog, k1, BO.

TAIL FEATHERS (work each tail feather in a different color; make 6)

Beginning at top of feather (ball), CO 6. Join in a round.

Round 1 kfb around: 12 sts
Rounds 2-5 knit
Round 6 k2tog around: 6 sts

Leaving sts on the needle(s), lightly stuff.

Round 7 k2tog around, onto one needle: 3 sts
Round 8 k1, kfb, k1: 4 sts.

Continue in 4-st I-cord for 6 rows. BO. Repeat for other tail feathers.

FEET AND LEGS (make 2)

With blue, CO 6. Join in a round.

Round 1 kfb around: 12 sts
Rounds 2-5 knit
Round 6 k2tog around: 6 sts.

Leaving sts on the needle(s), lightly stuff foot.

Round 7 k2tog around, onto one needle: 3 sts

Continue in 3-st I-cord until leg measures ~2". BO.

Repeat for second foot and leg.

ASSEMBLY AND FINISHING

Sew legs to body on either side of front as shown. With yellow, make 3 sts for toes (a long stitch at center and one shorter, slanted stitch on each side of center toe). With black, make 2 French knot eyes. Attach tail feathers as shown.

Penguin

Yarn
Brown Sheep Lamb's Pride Worsted colors M05 (Onyx), M174 (Wild Mustard), and M11 (White Frost)

Yardage
Black, 48 yds
White, 10 yds
Yellow, 10 yds

Measurements
Penguin is 5-1/2″ tall.

Notes
1. Please read the Read Me First chapter, pp. 6-16 before you begin.

Instructions
With black, work basic bottom, p. 11, through round 10: 48 sts.

Body (continue working in the round)

Rounds 1-10 knit
Round 11 *k2, ssk, k8, k2tog, k2, rep from * around: 42 sts
Rounds 12-15 knit
Round 16 *k2, ssk, k6, k2tog, k2, rep from * around: 36 sts
Rounds 17-20 knit
Round 21 *k2, ssk, k4, k2tog, k2, rep from * around: 30 sts
Rounds 22-25 knit
Round 26 *k2, ssk, k2, k2tog, k2, rep from * around: 24 sts
Round 27 knit

Round 28 *k2, ssk, rep from * around: 18 sts

Leaving sts on the needle(s), lightly stuff body.

Head (continue working in the round)

Rounds 1-10 knit

Leaving sts on the needle(s), lightly stuff head.

Round 11 k2tog around: 9 sts
Round 12 knit
Round 13 *k2tog, k1, rep from * around: 6 sts

Add stuffing as necessary. Break yarn, thread tail through remaining sts, pull up and weave through.

WHITE BREAST (worked flat)

With white, CO 8.

Row 1 purl
Row 2 *kfb, k1, rep from * around: 12 sts
Row 3 purl
Row 4 knit
Row 5 purl
Row 6 *kfb, k2, rep from * around: 16 sts
Rows 7-17 continue purling WS rows and knitting RS rows
Row 18 k2, ssk, k8, k2tog, k2: 14 sts
Rows 19-21 continue purling WS rows and knitting RS rows
Row 22 k2, ssk, k6, k2tog, k2: 12 sts
Rows 23-27 continue purling WS rows and knitting RS rows
Row 28 k2, ssk, k4, k2tog, k2: 10 sts
Rows 29-31 continue purling WS rows and knitting RS rows
Row 32 k2, ssk, k2, k2tog, k2: 8 sts
Rows 33-37 continue purling WS rows and knitting RS rows
Row 38 k2, ssk, k2tog, k2: 6 sts

BO.

FEET (worked flat, make 2)

With yellow, CO 13.

Row 1   k6, p1, k6
Row 2   k5, cdd, k5: 11 sts
Row 3   k5, p1, k5
Row 4   knit
Row 5   rep row 3
Row 6   k4, cdd, k4: 9 sts
Row 7   k4, p1, k4
Row 8   knit
Row 9   rep row 7
Row 10 k3, cdd, k3: 7 sts
Row 11 k3, p1, k3
Row 12 knit
Row 13 rep row 11
Row 14 k2, cdd, k2: 5 sts
Row 15 k2, p1, k2
Row 16 k1, cdd, k1: 3 sts
Row 17 k1, p1, k1
Row 18 cdd: 1 st

BO. Repeat for second foot.

BEAK (worked flat, make 2)

With yellow, CO 4.

Row 1 purl
Row 2 k1, sl1, k1, psso, k1: 3 sts
Row 3 purl
Row 4 sl2, k1, p2sso: 1 st

BO. Repeat for second half of beak.

WINGS (worked flat, make 2)

With black, CO 4.

Row 1 knit
Row 2 k1, [kfb] twice, k1: 6 sts
Row 3 knit
Row 4 k2, [kfb] twice, k2: 8 sts
Rows 5-34 knit

BO. Repeat for second wing.

ASSEMBLY AND FINISHING

Sew white breast to front of body. Sew the BO edge of wings to sides of body. Sew both halves of beak to face, one above the other, wrong sides facing. With white, embroider 2 lazy-daisy stitch eyes. With black, make a French knot inside each white outline. Using straight stitches and yellow and white, make "feathery" accents around eyes as shown.

Timeless Toys 47

Toucan

Yarn

Brown Sheep Lamb's Pride Worsted colors M05 (Onyx) and M174 (Wild Mustard)

Noro Kureyon
(in any colorway that pleases)

Yardage

Black, 50 yds
Yellow, 5 yds
Self-striping, 5 yds

Measurements

Toucan is 5-1/2" tall.

Notes

1. Please read the Read Me First chapter, pp. 6-16 before you begin.

Instructions

With black, work bird bottom, p. 11: 42 sts.

Body (continue working in the round)

Rounds 1-6 knit
Round 7 k9, k2tog, k4, ssk, k8, k2tog, k4, ssk, k9: 38 sts
Rounds 8-11 knit
Round 12 k8, k2tog, k4, ssk, k6, k2tog, k4, ssk, k8: 34 sts
Rounds 13-16 knit
Round 17 k7, k2tog, k4, ssk, k4, k2tog, k4, ssk, k7: 30 sts
Rounds 18-20 knit
Round 21 *k2, ssk, k2, k2tog, k2, rep from * around: 24 sts
Round 22 [k2tog] 4 times, ssk, k4, k2tog, [ssk] 4 times: 14 sts

Leaving sts on the needle(s), lightly stuff body.

HEAD (continue working in the round)

k4, turn (back neck is worked flat, beginning with 8 sts at center back)

Row 1 sl1, pfb, [p1, pfb] 3 times: 12 sts
Row 2 sl1, k11
Row 3 sl1, p11
Rows 4,6,8,10 rep row 2
Rows 5,7,9 rep row 3

SHAPE CROWN (short rows)

Row 1 sl1, p6, p2tog, p1, turn
Row 2 sl1, k3, ssk, k1, turn
Row 3 sl1, p4, p2tog, p1, turn
Row 4 sl1, k5, ssk, k1

Eight (8) sts remain in crown.

From the RS, with gold, pick up and knit 5 sts along left side of neck; k across 6 sts at center front; pick up and knit 5 sts along right side of neck; k4. Round (24 sts) now begins at center of crown.

FACE (worked in the round)

Round 1 knit
Round 2 ssk, k5, k2tog, k6, ssk, k5, k2tog: 20 sts
Round 3 knit
Round 4 ssk, k3, k2tog, ssk, k2, k2tog, ssk, k3, k2tog: 14 sts
Round 5 knit
Round 6 ssk, k10, k2tog: 12 sts

Leaving sts on the needle(s), lightly stuff head.

Round 7 k2tog around: 6 sts

Break yarn, thread tail through remaining sts, pull up and weave through.

BEAK (worked as a separate piece)

The beak is worked from self-striping yarn. To make stripes on the beak, work from both ends of the ball, alternating every two rows.

CO 15.

Row 1 k6, cdd, k6: 13 sts
Row 2 purl
Row 3 k5, cdd, k5: 11 sts
Row 4 purl
Row 5 k4, cdd, k4: 9 sts
Row 6 purl

Join in a round and continue working in the round.

Rounds 1-2 knit
Round 3 k6, wrap the next st and turn, p3, wrap the next st and turn, k4, knitting in the wrap with the last st, wrap the next st and turn, p5, purling in the wrap with the last st, wrap the next st and turn, k7, knitting in the wrap with the 6th st
Rounds 4-7 knit
Round 8 *k2tog, k1, rep from * around: 6 sts

Rounds 9-11 knit
Round 12 k2tog around: 3 sts

Break yarn, thread tail through remaining sts, pull up and weave through. Stuff firmly.

FEET (make 2)

With black, CO 6. Join in a round.

Round 1 kfb around: 12 sts
Rounds 2-5 knit
Round 6 k2tog around: 6 sts

Lightly stuff. Break yarn, thread tail through remaining sts, pull up and weave through. Repeat for second foot.

ASSEMBLY AND FINISHING

Sew feet to body on either side of front as shown. With yellow, make 3 sts for toes (a long stitch at center and one shorter, slanted stitch on each side of center toe). Attach beak to face. With black, make 2 French knot eyes. Cut four 6" lengths of black and attach as for fringe at tail (making tail feathers, as shown). Trim tail feathers to 2".

Heartland

I spent my early childhood in The Heartland with 4H Club, square dancing on Saturday nights, and school picnics that always included hayrides. This collection is definitely close to my heart!

Cow and Calf

YARN
Brown Sheep Lamb's Pride Worsted colors M175 (Bronze Patina), M115 (Oatmeal), and M05 (Onyx)

YARDAGE
Brown: Cow, 75 yds; Calf, 35 yds
Beige: Cow, 12 yds
Black: Cow, 1 yd; Calf, 1 yd

MEASUREMENTS
Cow is 7" tall; calf is 5" tall.

NOTES
1. Please read the Read Me First chapter, pp. 6-16 before you begin.

COW INSTRUCTIONS
Work basic bottom, p. 11, through round 15: 60 sts.

BODY (continue working in the round)

Rounds 1-3 knit
Round 4 *k2, ssk, k12, k2tog, k2, rep from * around: 54 sts
Rounds 5-7 knit
Round 8 *k2, ssk, k10, k2tog, k2, rep from * around: 48 sts
Rounds 9-18 knit
Round 19 *k2, ssk, k8, k2tog, k2, rep from * around: 42 sts
Rounds 20-24 knit
Round 25 *k2, ssk, k6, k2tog, k2, rep from * around: 36 sts
Rounds 26-28 knit
Round 29 *k2, ssk, k4, k2tog, k2, rep from * around: 30 sts
Rounds 30-32 knit
Round 33 *k2, ssk, k2, k2tog, k2, rep from * around: 24 sts
Round 34 knit

Leaving sts on the needle(s), stuff body.

Round 35 k2tog around: 12 sts

BACK NECK (worked flat over 8 sts at center back; round begins at center of these sts)

Knit the first 4 sts of the next round. Turn. *pfb, p1, rep from * three times more: 12 sts. Turn.

Row 1 sl1, k11
Row 2 sl1, p11

Rep rows 1 and 2 a total of 5 times, then rep row 1 once more (11 rows total).

SHAPE CROWN (short rows)

Row 1 sl1, p6, p2tog, p1, turn
Row 2 sl1, k3, ssk, k1, turn
Row 3 sl1, p4, p2tog, p1, turn
Row 4 sl1, k5, ssk, k1, turn
Row 5 sl1, p5, p2tog, turn
Row 6 k5, ssk

Six (6) sts remain in crown.

From the RS, pick up and knit 8 sts along the left side of neck; knit 4 sts at center front neck; pick up and knit 8 sts along the right side of neck; knit 3 sts from crown. Round (26 sts) now begins at center crown.

FACE (worked in the round)

Round 1 k11, [k2tog] twice, k11: 24 sts
Round 2 knit
Round 3 k3, [k2tog] 4 times, k2, [k2tog] 4 times, k3: 16 sts
Round 4 knit
Round 5 k1, k2tog, k2, k2tog, k2, k2tog, k2, k2tog, k1: 12 sts
Rounds 6-8 knit

Leaving sts on the needle(s), stuff neck, head, and face.

Round 9 *k1, k2tog, k1, rep from * around: 9 sts
Round 10 knit
Round 11 k1, [kfb] 2 times, k3, [kfb] 2 times, k1: 13 sts
Round 12 knit
Round 13 k1, [k2tog] 2 times, k3, [k2tog] 2 times, k1: 9 sts.

Leaving sts on the needle(s), stuff nose. Break yarn, thread tail through remaining sts, pull up and weave through.

EARS (worked flat, make 2)

CO 6.

Row 1 purl
Row 2 k2, [kfb] twice, k2: 8 sts
Row 3 purl
Row 4 k2, ssk, k2tog, k2: 6 sts
Row 5 purl
Row 6 k1, ssk, k2tog, k1: 4 sts
Row 7 purl
Row 8 ssk, k2tog: 2 sts

BO. Repeat for second ear.

Timeless Toys

Tail

With brown, work 3-st I-cord for 2″. Cut three 6″ strands of beige and thread through ending 3 sts of I-cord, with 3″ of fringe on each side. Use an overhand knot to tie the tail fringe and secure the I-cord. Trim to irregular lengths as shown.

Udder (worked flat)

Bag:

With beige, CO 7.

Row 1 purl
Row 2 kfb, k4, kfb, k1: 9 sts
Row 3 purl
Row 4 kfb, k6, kfb, k1: 11 sts
Row 5 purl
Row 6 knit
Row 7 purl
Row 8 ssk, k7, k2tog: 9 sts
Row 9 purl
Row 10 ssk, k5, k2tog: 7 sts

BO.

Teats: (make 4)

With beige, CO 3. Work in 3-st I-cord for 3 rows.

Row 4 k2tog, k1: 2 sts

BO. Repeat for other 3 teats. Sew teats to bag in 2 rows.

Legs and feet (worked in the round, make 4)

With brown, CO 9.

Rounds 1-20 knit
Round 21 k4, kfb, k4: 10 sts
Rounds 22-26 knit
Round 27 k2tog around: 5 sts

Break yarn, thread tail through remaining sts, pull up and weave through. Stuff foot, leaving leg unstuffed. With black, make a single straight stitch to delineate cleft hoof as shown. Repeat for other 3 legs.

Assembly and finishing

Sew ears to either side of crown as shown. With black, make satin stitch eyes and lazy-daisy stitch nostrils as shown. Sew udder to body as shown, adding a bit of stuffing between the body and the bag. Sew legs and feet to front of body as shown. Sew tail to back of body as shown.

Calf Instructions

Work basic bottom, p. 11, through round 10: 48 sts.

Body (continue working in the round)

Rounds 1-3 knit
Round 4 *k2, ssk, k8, k2tog, k2, rep from * around: 42 sts
Rounds 5-7 knit
Round 8 *k2, ssk, k6, k2tog, k2, rep from * around: 36 sts
Rounds 9-15 knit
Round 16 *k2, ssk, k4, k2tog, k2, rep from * around: 30 sts
Rounds 17-18 knit
Round 19 *k2, ssk, k2, k2tog, k2, rep from * around: 24 sts
Round 20 knit

Leaving sts on the needle(s), stuff body.

Round 21 k2tog around: 12 sts
Round 22 knit

Back neck (worked flat over 6 sts at center back; round begins at center of these sts)

Knit the first 3 sts of the next round. Turn. p1, pfb, p2, pfb, p1: 8 sts. Turn.

Row 1 sl1, k7
Row 2 sl1, p7

Rep rows 1 and 2 a total of 4 times, then rep row 1 once more (9 rows total).

Shape crown (short rows)

Row 1 sl1, p3, p2tog, p1, turn
Row 2 sl1, k1, ssk, k1, turn
Row 3 sl1, p2, p2tog, turn
Row 4 k3, ssk

Four (4) sts remain in crown.

From the RS, pick up and knit 6 sts along the left side of neck; ssk, k2, k2tog at center front neck; pick up and knit 6 sts along the right side of neck; knit 2 sts from crown. Round (20 sts) now begins at center crown.

FACE (worked in the round)

Round 1 k8, ssk, k2tog, k8: 18 sts
Round 2 knit
Round 3 k2, [k2tog] 3 times, k2, [k2tog] 3 times, k2: 12 sts
Round 4 knit

Leaving sts on the needle(s), stuff neck, head, and face.

Round 5 k2tog, k1, k2tog, k2, k2tog, k1, k2tog: 8 sts
Round 6 knit
Round 7 k1, kfb, k4, kfb, k1: 10 sts
Round 8 knit
Round 9 k1, k2tog, k4, k2tog, k1: 8 sts

Leaving sts on the needle(s), stuff nose. Break yarn, thread tail through remaining sts, pull up and weave through.

EARS (worked flat, make 2)

CO 4.

Row 1 purl
Row 2 k1, [kfb] twice, k1: 6 sts
Row 3 purl
Row 4 k1, ssk, k2tog, k1: 4 sts
Row 5 purl
Row 6 ssk, k2tog: 2 sts

BO. Repeat for second ear.

TAIL

With brown, work 3-st I-cord for 1-1/2". Cut three 5" strands of beige and thread through ending 3 sts of I-cord, with 2-1/2" of fringe on each side. Use an overhand knot to tie the tail fringe and secure the I-cord. Trim to irregular lengths as shown.

LEGS AND FEET (make 4)

CO 4. Work in 4-st I-cord for 15 rows.

Row 16 k1, [kfb] twice, k1: 6 sts

Work 2 more rows with 6 sts. Break yarn, thread tail through remaining sts, pull up and weave through. With black, make a single straight stitch to delineate cleft hoof as shown. Repeat for other 3 legs.

ASSEMBLY AND FINISHING

Sew ears to either side of crown as shown. With black, make satin stitch eyes and straight stitch nostrils as shown. Sew legs and feet to front of body as shown. Sew tail to back of body as shown.

Ewe & Lamb

Yarn

Brown Sheep Lamb's Pride Worsted colors M10 (Creme) and M05 (Onyx)

Plymouth Yarn Select Boucle Merino Superwash (sheepy yarn), color 1

Yardage

Sheepy yarn (textured): Ewe, 55 yds; Lamb, 25 yds
Smooth yarn: Ewe, 45 yds; Lamb, 35 yds
Smooth yarn in contrasting color for features: Ewe, 3 yds; Lamb, 3 yds

Measurements

Ewe is 7" tall; lamb is 5" tall.

Notes

1. Please read the Read Me First chapter, pp. 6-16 before you begin.

Ewe Instructions

With sheepy yarn, work basic bottom, p. 11, through round 15: 60 sts.

Body (continue working in the round)

Rounds 1-4 knit
Round 5 *k2, ssk, k12, k2tog, k2, rep from * around: 54 sts
Rounds 6-8 knit
Round 9 *k2, ssk, k10, k2tog, k2, rep from * around: 48 sts
Rounds 10-12 knit
Round 13 *k2, ssk, k8, k2tog, k2, rep from * around: 42 sts
Rounds 14-15 knit
Round 16 *k2, ssk, k6, k2tog, k2, rep from * around: 36 sts
Rounds 17-18 knit
Round 19 *k2, ssk, k4, k2tog, k2, rep from * around: 30 sts
Rounds 20-21 knit
Round 22 *k2, ssk, k2, k2tog, k2, rep from * around: 24 sts

Leaving sts on the needle(s), stuff body.

Round 23 k2tog around: 12 sts

Back neck (worked flat over 8 sts at center back; round begins at center of these sts)

Knit the first 4 sts of the next round. Turn. *pfb, p1, rep from * three times more: 12 sts. Turn.

Row 1 sl1, k11
Row 2 sl1, p11

Repeat rows 1 and 2 a total of 5 times, then rep row 1 once more (11 rows total).

Timeless Toys 57

SHAPE CROWN (short rows)

Row 1 sl1, p6, p2tog, p1, turn
Row 2 sl1, k3, ssk, k1, turn
Row 3 sl1, p4, p2tog, p1, turn
Row 4 sl1, k5, ssk, k1, turn
Row 5 sl1, p5, p2tog, turn
Row 6 k5, ssk

Six (6) sts remain in crown.

Break sheepy yarn. With smooth yarn, from the RS, pick up and knit 8 sts along the left side of neck; knit 4 sts at center front neck; pick up and knit 8 sts along the right side of neck; knit 3 sts from crown. Round (26 sts) now begins at center crown.

FACE (worked in the round)

Round 1 k11, [k2tog] twice, k11: 24 sts
Round 2 knit
Round 3 k3, [k2tog] 4 times, k2, [k2tog] 4 times, k3: 16 sts
Round 4 knit
Round 5 k1, k2tog, k2, k2tog, k2, k2tog, k2, k2tog, k1: 12 sts
Rounds 6-8 knit

Leaving sts on the needle(s), stuff neck, head, and face.

Round 9 *k1, k2tog, k1, rep from * around: 9 sts
Rounds 10-12 knit

Leaving sts on the needle(s), stuff nose. Break yarn, thread tail through remaining sts, pull up and weave through.

EARS (worked flat, make 2)

With smooth yarn, CO 3.

Row 1 purl
Row 2 [kfb] twice, k1: 5 sts
Row 3 purl
Row 4 k1, [kfb] twice, k2: 7 sts
Row 5 purl
Row 6 k1, ssk, k1, k2tog, k1: 5 sts
Row 7 purl
Row 8 knit
Row 9 purl
Row 10 ssk, k1, k2tog: 3 sts
Row 11 purl
Row 12 ssk, k1: 2 sts

BO. Repeat for second ear.

TAIL (worked flat)

With sheepy yarn, CO 3.

Row 1 purl
Row 2 [kfb] twice, k1: 5 sts
Row 3 purl
Row 4 knit
Row 5 purl
Row 6 ssk, k1, k2tog: 3 sts
Row 7 purl
Row 8 ssk, k1: 2 sts

BO.

Lamb Instructions

With sheepy yarn, Work basic bottom, p. 11, through round 10: 48 sts.

Body (continue working in the round)

Rounds 1-4 knit
Round 5 *k2, ssk, k8, k2tog, k2, rep from * around: 42 sts
Rounds 6-7 knit
Round 8 *k2, ssk, k6, k2tog, k2, rep from * around: 36 sts
Rounds 9-10 knit
Round 11 *k2, ssk, k4, k2tog, k2, rep from * around: 30 sts
Rounds 12-13 knit
Round 14 *k2, ssk, k2, k2tog, k2, rep from * around: 24 sts
Rounds 15-17 knit

Leaving sts on the needle(s), stuff body.

Round 18 k2tog around: 12 sts

Back neck (worked flat over 6 sts at center back; round begins at center of these sts)

Knit the first 3 sts of the next round. Turn. p1, pfb, p2, pfb, p1: 8 sts. Turn.

Row 1 sl1, k7
Row 2 sl1, p7

Repeat rows 1 and 2 a total of 4 times, then rep row 1 once more (9 rows total).

Legs and feet (worked in the round, make 4)

With sheepy yarn, CO 9. Join in a round and knit 6 rounds.

Switch to smooth yarn, and continue:

Rounds 1-18 knit
Round 19 k3, kfb, k4, kfb: 11 sts
Rounds 20-23 knit
Round 24 k3, k2tog, k4, k2tog: 9 sts
Round 25 knit

Break yarn, thread tail through remaining sts, pull up and weave through. Stuff foot, leaving leg unstuffed. With contrasting color, sew a loop from the back of the foot at center, over the toe, and back to center back. Pull up tight and weave through. Repeat for each of three other legs and feet.

Assembly and finishing

Sew ears in place on either side of crown. With contrasting yarn, make eyes with lazy-daisy stitch. Make nose with straight stitches. With sheepy yarn, embroider 4 or 5 loops on crown, between ears. Sew tail to bottom of back. Sew legs to body as shown.

SHAPE CROWN (short rows)

Row 1 sl1, p3, p2tog, p1, turn
Row 2 sl1, k1, ssk, k1, turn
Row 3 sl1, p2, p2tog, turn
Row 4 k3, ssk

Four (4) sts remain in crown.

Break sheepy yarn. With smooth yarn, from the RS, pick up and knit 6 sts along the left side of neck; ssk, k2, k2tog at center front neck; pick up and knit 6 sts along the right side of neck; knit 2 sts from crown. Round (20 sts) now begins at center crown.

FACE (worked in the round)

Round 1 k8, ssk, k2tog, k8: 18 sts
Round 2 knit
Round 3 k2, [k2tog] 3 times, k2, [k2tog] 3 times, k2: 12 sts
Round 4 knit

Leaving sts on the needle(s), stuff neck, head, and face.

Round 5 k2tog, k1, k2tog, k2, k2tog, k1, k2tog: 8 sts
Rounds 6-7 knit

Leaving sts on the needle(s), stuff nose. Break yarn, thread tail through remaining sts, pull up and weave through.

EARS (worked flat, make 2)

With smooth yarn, CO 3.

Row 1 purl
Row 2 [kfb] twice, k1: 5 sts
Row 3 purl
Row 4 ssk, k1, k2tog: 3 sts
Row 5 purl
Row 6 ssk, k1: 2 sts

BO. Repeat for second ear.

TAIL

With sheepy yarn, CO 3. Work in 3-st I-cord for 3 rows. BO.

LEGS AND FEET (worked in the round, make 4)

With sheepy yarn, CO 6. Join in a round. Knit 4 rounds. Switch to smooth yarn and continue:

Rounds 1-18 knit
Round 19 k2, kfb, k2, kfb: 8 sts
Rounds 20-23 knit
Round 24 k2, k2tog, k2, k2tog: 6 sts
Round 25 knit

Break yarn, thread tail through remaining sts, pull up and weave through. Stuff foot, leaving leg unstuffed. With contrasting color, sew a loop from the back of the foot at center, over the toe, and back to center back. Pull up tight and tie off. Repeat for each of three other legs and feet.

ASSEMBLY AND FINISHING

Sew ears in place on either side of crown. With contrasting yarn, make eyes with lazy-daisy stitch. Make nose with straight stitches. With sheepy yarn, embroider 3 or 4 loops on crown, between ears. Sew tail to bottom of back. Sew legs to body as shown.

Goose & Goslings

Yarn

Brown Sheep Lamb's Pride Worsted
For goose: colors M11 (White Frost), M110 (Orange You Glad), and M05 (Onyx)

For goslings: colors M13 (Sun Yellow), M174 (Wild Mustard), and M05 (Onyx)

Filatura Di Crosa Baby Kid Extra color 520 (Butter Yellow)

Yardage

Goose: 55 yds white, 10 yds orange, and 1/2 yd black

Goslings (each): 28 yds each of Lamb's Pride and Baby Kid Extra yellow (held together), 10 yds gold, and 1/2 yd black

Measurements

Goose is 10" tall; goslings are ~7" tall.

Notes

1. Please read the Read Me First chapter, pp. 6-16 before you begin.

Goose Instructions

With white, work large bird bottom, p. 11: 52 sts.

Body (continue working in the round)

Round 1 k23, [kfb] 6 times, k23: 58 sts
Rounds 2-7 knit
Round 8 k2tog, k54, ssk: 56 sts
Round 9 knit
Round 10 k2tog, k52, ssk: 54 sts
Rounds 11-13 knit
Round 14 *k2, ssk, k10, k2tog, k2, rep from * around: 48 sts
Rounds 15-19 knit
Round 20 *k2, ssk, k8, k2tog, k2, rep from * around: 42 sts
Rounds 21-25 knit
Round 26 *k2, ssk, k6, k2tog, k2, rep from * around: 36 sts
Rounds 27-29 knit
Round 30 *k2, ssk, k4, k2tog, k2, rep from * around: 30 sts

Rounds 31-33 knit
Round 34 *k2, ssk, k2, k2tog, k2, rep from * around: 24 sts
Round 35 knit

Leaving sts on the needle(s), stuff body.

NECK (continue working in the round)

Round 1 k2tog, k16, wrap the next st and turn; p12, wrap the next st and turn; k12, knitting the wrap in with the next st, k3, ssk
Round 2 k4, knit in the wrap with the next st, k17: 22 sts
Round 3 knit
Round 4 k2tog, k15, wrap the next st and turn; k12, wrap the next st and turn; k12, knitting the wrap in with its corresponding st, k2, ssk
Round 5 k3, knit the next st with its wrap, k16: 20 sts
Round 6 knit
Round 7 k2, ssk, k4, ssk, k2tog, k4, k2tog, k2: 16 sts

Leaving sts on the needle(s), stuff lower neck.

Round 8 k4, wrap the next st and turn, p8, wrap the next st and turn, k4
Round 9 k4, knit the next st with its wrap, k2, k2tog, k2, knit the next st with its wrap, k4: 15 sts
Round 10 rep round 8
Round 11 k4, knit the next st with its wrap, k5, knit the next st with its wrap, k4
Rounds 12-13 rep rounds 8 and 11
Rounds 14-15 rep rounds 8 and 11
Round 16 k4, [kfb] twice, k3, [kfb] twice, k4: 19 sts

CROWN AND HEAD (continue working in the round with short rows)

Round 1 k3, wrap the next st and turn; p6, wrap the next st and turn; k5, wrap the next st and turn; p4, wrap the next st and turn, k2
Round 2 knit, knitting in wraps with their corresponding sts
Rounds 3-4 knit
Round 5 k4, [ssk] twice, k3, [k2tog] twice, k4: 15 sts
Round 6 knit

Leaving sts on the needle(s), stuff crown and head. Break off white.

BEAK (continue working in the round)

Continue with orange:

Round 1 knit
Round 2 k3, ssk, k2tog, k1, ssk, k2tog, k3: 11 sts
Rounds 3-7 knit
Round 8 k2, ssk, k3, k2tog, k2: 9 sts
Rounds 9-10 knit

Leaving sts on the needle(s), stuff neck, head, and face.

Round 11 *k1, k2tog, rep from * around: 6 sts
Rounds 12-14 knit

Leaving sts on the needle(s), stuff beak. Break yarn, thread tail through remaining sts, pull up and weave through.

FEET AND LEGS (feet worked flat in garter stitch and finished with 3-st I-cord leg, make 2)

With orange, CO 21.

Row 1 k1, sl1, k8, p1, k8, sl1, k1
Row 2 k9, cdd, k9: 19 sts
Row 3 k1, sl1, k7, p1, k7, sl1, k1
Row 4 k8, cdd, k8: 17 sts
Row 5 k1, sl1, k6, p1, k6, sl1, k1
Row 6 k7, cdd, k7: 15 sts
Row 7 k1, sl1, k5, p1, k5, sl1, k1
Row 8 k6, cdd, k6: 13 sts
Row 9 k1, sl1, k4, p1, k4, sl1, k1
Row 10 k5, cdd, k5: 11 sts
Row 11 k1, sl1, k3, p1, k3, sl1, k1
Row 12 k4, cdd, k4: 9 sts
Row 13 k1, sl1, k2, p1, k2, sl1, k1
Row 14 k3, cdd, k3: 7 sts
Row 15 k1, sl1, k1, p1, k1, sl1, k1
Row 16 k2, cdd, k2: 5 sts
Row 17 k1, sl1, p1, sl1, k1
Row 18 k1, cdd, k1: 3 sts

Do not turn work. Continue in 3-st I-cord until leg above foot is 2" long. BO.

Top of leg: This is a separate piece to be joined with leg when attaching to body.

With white, CO 4. Work in 4-st I-cord for 10-12 rows. BO.

Repeat for second foot and leg.

ASSEMBLY AND FINISHING

Form a circle with the top of leg piece around the top of the I-cord leg. Stitch in place. Stitch this circle to the bottom of the goose. Repeat for second leg. With black, make 2 lazy-daisy stitch eyes.

GOSLING INSTRUCTIONS

Holding both yellow yarns together throughout, work basic bottom, p. 11, through round 7: 36 sts.

SHAPE TAIL

Work as for bird bottom, p. 11, through row 7. Finish by knitting the next round: k4, knit the next st with its wrap, k20, knit the next st with its wrap, k4. Thirty (30) sts remain in the round.

BODY (continue working in the round)

Round 1 k13, [kfb] 4 times, k13: 34 sts
Rounds 2-4 knit
Round 5 k2tog, k30, ssk: 32 sts
Round 6 knit
Round 7 k2tog, k28, ssk: 30 sts
Rounds 8-10 knit
Round 11 *k2, ssk, k2, k2tog, k2, rep

Timeless Toys

from * around: 24 sts
Rounds 12-16 knit
Round 17 *k2, ssk, k2tog, k2, rep from * around: 18 sts
Rounds 18-20 knit

Leaving sts on the needle(s), stuff body.

Round 21 *k1, ssk, k2tog, k1, rep from * around: 12 sts
Round 22 knit

NECK (continue working in the round)

Round 1 k9, wrap the next st and turn; p6, wrap the next st and turn; k6, knitting the wrap in with the next st, k2, ssk
Round 2 k2, knit in the wrap with the next st, k9
Round 3 knit
Rounds 4-6 rep rounds 1-3

Leaving sts on the needle(s), stuff lower neck.

Gosling 1 (looking forward):

Rounds 7-12 knit
Round 13 k5, k2tog, k5: 11 sts
Round 14 k3, wrap the next st and turn; p6, wrap the next st and turn; p3
Round 15 k3, knit the next st with its wrap; k3, knit the next st with its wrap; k3
Round 16-17 rep rounds 14-15
Round 18-19 rep round 14-15

Leaving sts on the needle(s), stuff neck.

Gosling 2 (looking up):

Rounds 7-16 knit
Round 17 k3, wrap the next st and turn; p6, wrap the next st and turn; p3
Round 18 k3, knit the next st with its wrap; k4, knit the next st with its wrap; k3
Round 19 k5, k2tog, k5: 11 sts

Leaving sts on the needle(s), stuff neck.

CROWN AND HEAD (both versions, continue working in the round with short rows)

Round 1 k2, wrap the next st and turn; p4, wrap the next st and turn; k3, wrap the next st and turn; p2, wrap the next st and turn; k1
Round 2 knit, knitting in wraps with their corresponding sts
Round 3 k3, [kfb] twice, k1, [kfb] twice, k3: 15 sts
Rounds 4-5 knit
Round 6 k2tog, k1, ssk, k2tog, k1, ssk, k2tog, k1, ssk: 9 sts

Leaving sts on the needle(s), stuff crown and head. Break off yellow.

BEAK (continue working in the round)

Continue with gold:

Rounds 1-5 knit

Leaving sts on the needle(s), stuff beak.

Round 6 *k2tog, k1, rep from * around: 6 sts.

Break yarn, thread tail through remaining sts, pull up and weave through.

FEET AND LEGS (feet worked flat

in garter stitch and finished with 3-st I-cord leg, make 2)

With gold, CO 15.

Row 1 k1, sl1, k5, p1, k5, sl1, k1
Row 2 k6, cdd, k6: 13 sts
Row 3 k1, sl1, k4, p1, k4, sl1, k1
Row 4 k5, cdd, k5: 11 sts
Row 5 k1, sl1, k3, p1, k3, sl1, k1
Row 6 k4, cdd, k4: 9 sts
Row 7 k1, sl1, k2, p1, k2, sl1, k1
Row 8 k3, cdd, k3: 7 sts
Row 9 k1, sl1, k1, p1, k1, sl1, k1
Row 10 k2, cdd, k2: 5 sts
Row 11 k1, sl1, p1, sl1, k1
Row 12 k1, cdd, k1: 3 sts

Do not turn. Continue in I-cord, working the first row as follows: ssk, k1: 2 sts. Continue in 2-st I-cord until leg above foot is 1-1/2" long. BO.

Top of leg: This is a separate piece to be joined with leg when attaching to body.

With yellow, CO 4. Work in 4-st I-cord for 8-10 rows. BO.

Repeat for second foot and leg.

ASSEMBLY AND FINISHING

Form a circle with the top of leg piece around the top of the I-cord leg. Stitch in place. Stitch this circle to the bottom of the gosling. Repeat for second leg. With black, make 2 duplicate stitch eyes. Use a small brush (like a toothbrush) to fluff out the mohair.

Timeless Toys

Hen & Chicks

Yarn

Brown Sheep Lamb's Pride Worsted
For hen: colors M10 (Creme), M155 (Lemon Drop), M197 (Red Hot Passion), and M05 (Onyx)

For chicks: colors M13 (Sun Yellow), M155 (Lemon Drop), and M05 (Onyx)

Filatura Di Crosa Baby Kid Extra color 520 (Butter Yellow)

Yardage

Hen: 50 yds cream, 12 yds red, 1 yd dark yellow, and 1/2 yd black

Chicks (each): 6 yds each of Lamb's Pride and Baby Kid Extra yellow (held together), 1/4 yd dark yellow, and 1/2 yd black

Measurements

Hen is ~4" tall; chicks are ~1" tall.

Notes

1. Please read the Read Me First chapter, pp. 6-16 before you begin.

Hen Instructions

With cream, work large bird bottom, p. 11: 52 sts.

Body (continue working in the round)

Round 1 knit
Round 2 k2tog, k48, ssk: 50 sts
Round 3 knit
Round 4 k2tog, k46, ssk: 48 sts
Rounds 5-14 knit
Round 15 k34, wrap the next st and turn; p20, wrap the next st and turn; k20, knit the wrap with the next st, k13
Round 16 k13, knit the wrap with the next st, k34
Rounds 17-18 rep rounds 15-16
Rounds 19-20 rep rounds 15-16
Round 21 *k2, ssk, k8, k2tog, k2, rep from * around: 42 sts
Round 22 knit
Round 23 *k2, ssk, k6, k2tog, k2, rep from * around: 36 sts
Round 24 knit
Round 25 *k2, ssk, k4, k2tog, k2, rep from * around: 30 sts
Round 26 knit
Round 27 *k2, ssk, k2, k2tog, k2, rep from * around: 24 sts
Round 28 knit

Leaving sts on the needle(s), stuff body.

Round 29 *k2, ssk, k2tog, k2, rep from * around: 18 sts

HEAD (continue working in the round)

Rounds 1-3 knit

Switch to red.

Rounds 4-9 knit
Round 10 k2tog around: 9 sts

Leaving sts on the needle(s), stuff neck and head. Break yarn, thread tail through remaining sts, pull up and weave through.

COMB (make 5)

With red, CO 3. Work 2 rows in 3-st I-cord.

Row 3 slip the first 2 sts together as if to knit, k1, p2sso: 1 st

BO. Rep 4 times more (5 comb segments in total).

BEAK (worked flat)

With dark yellow, CO 3.

Row 1 knit
Row 2 purl
Row 3 slip the first 2 sts together as if to knit, k1, p2sso: 1 st

BO.

ASSEMBLY AND FINISHING

Sew comb segments and beak to head as shown. With black, make straight stitch eyes as shown. With red, sew 4 short loops to neck as shown (for waddle).

Chick Instructions

Use one strand of light yellow and one strand of kid mohair held together, throughout. Work basic bottom, p. 11, through round 5: 24 sts.

Shape tail (short rows at center back)

Row 1 k1, ssk, k1, turn
Row 2 sl1, p3, p2tog, p1, turn
Row 3 sl1, k4, ssk, k1, wrap the next st and turn
Row 4 p5, p2tog, wrap the next st and turn
Row 5 k3 (to center back)

Finish by knitting the next round: k3, knit the next st with its wrap, k12, knit the next st with its wrap, k3. Twenty (20) sts remain in the round.

Body (continue working in the round)

Round 1 knit
Round 2 k2tog, k16, ssk: 18 sts
Round 3 knit
Round 4 k2tog, k14, ssk: 16 sts
Rounds 5-7 knit

Leaving sts on the needle(s), stuff body.

Head (continue working in the round)

Round 1 k1, k2tog, k3, ssk, k2tog, k3, ssk, k1: 12 sts
Rounds 2-3 knit
Round 4 k2tog around: 6 sts

Leaving sts on the needle(s), stuff head. Break yarn, thread tail through remaining sts, pull up and weave through.

Finishing

With dark yellow, attach a short strand to front of face as fringe; trim short as shown. With black, make straight stitch eyes as shown. Use a small brush (like a toothbrush) to fluff out the mohair.

Sow and Piglets

YARN
Brown Sheep Lamb's Pride Worsted colors M34 (Victorian Pink) and M175 (Bronze Patina)

YARDAGE
Pink: Sow, 85 yds; Piglets (each), 45 yds
Brown for features: Sow, 2 yds; Piglets (each), 2 yds

MEASUREMENTS
Sow is 7" long; piglets are ~4" long.

NOTES
1. Please read the Read Me First chapter, pp. 6-16 before you begin.

SOW INSTRUCTIONS
Work basic bottom, p. 11, through round 15: 60 sts.

BODY (continue working in the round)

Rounds 1-8 knit
Round 9 *k2, ssk, k12, k2tog, k2, rep from * around: 54 sts
Rounds 10-14 knit
Round 15 *k2, ssk, k10, k2tog, k2, rep from * around: 48 sts
Rounds 16-20 knit
Round 21 *k2, ssk, k8, k2tog, k2, rep from * around: 42 sts
Rounds 22-24 knit
Round 25 *k2, ssk, k6, k2tog, k2, rep from * around: 36 sts
Rounds 26-28 knit
Round 29 *k2, ssk, k4, k2tog, k2, rep from * around: 30 sts
Round 30 knit
Round 31 *k2, ssk, k2, k2tog, k2, rep from * around: 24 sts
Round 32 knit
Round 33 k10, ssk, k2tog, k10: 22 sts

Leaving sts on the needle(s), stuff body.

SHAPE CROWN (short rows)

Round 1 k6, wrap the next st and turn, p12, wrap the next st and turn, k10, wrap the next st and turn, p8, wrap the next st and turn, k4
Round 2 k9, knitting in wraps with corresponding sts, ssk, k2tog, k9, knitting in wraps with corresponding sts: 20 sts
Rounds 3-4 knit
Round 5 k6, ssk, k4, k2tog, k6: 18 sts
Round 6 knit
Round 7 k2tog, k14, ssk: 16 sts

Leaving sts on the needle(s), stuff neck and head.

SNOUT (worked in the round)

Round 1 k2tog, k12, ssk: 14 sts
Round 2 knit
Round 3 k3, ssk, k4, k2tog, k3: 12 sts
Round 4 knit

Leaving sts on the needle(s), stuff snout.

Round 5 k1, k2tog, k2, k2tog, k2, k2tog, k1: 9 sts

BO, but do not break yarn.

Pick up and knit 8 sts (one is left on the needle(s) from bind off), through the inside leg of the bound off sts: 9 sts. Gently add stuffing to snout if needed.

Break yarn, thread through 9 sts, and weave through, making a flat nose when pulling the tail through to the back.

EARS (worked flat, make 2)

CO 8.

Row 1 purl
Row 2 k2, ssk, k2tog, k2: 6 sts
Row 3 purl
Row 4 k1, ssk, k2tog, k1: 4 sts
Row 5 purl
Row 6 ssk, k2tog: 2 sts

BO. Repeat for second ear.

TAIL (worked in I-cord)

CO 3. Work in 3-st I-cord until ~3" long. BO, leaving an 8" tail. Use a running stitch with the yarn tail to weave over and under the "bars" between rows, sewing from the top of the I-cord to the CO edge. Pulling up on this yarn will encourage the tail to curl. Tie off.

LEGS AND FEET (worked in the round, make 4)

CO 9. Join in a round.

Rounds 1-18 knit
Round 19 k2, [kfb] 5 times, k2: 14 sts
Rounds 20-23 knit
Round 24 k2, [k2tog] 5 times, k2: 9 sts
Round 25 knit
Round 26 *k2tog, k1, rep from * around: 6 sts

Break yarn, thread tail through remaining sts, pull up and weave through. Stuff foot, leaving leg unstuffed. With brown yarn, sew a loop from the back of the foot at center, over the toe, and back to center back. Pull up tight and tie off. Repeat for each of three other legs and feet.

Assembly and finishing

Sew ears in place on either side of crown. With brown yarn, make duplicate stitch eyes. Make nostrils on snout end with straight stitches. Sew curly tail to bottom of back. Sew legs to body as shown.

Piglet Instructions

Work basic bottom, p. 11, through round 6: 36 sts.

Body (continue working in the round)

Rounds 1-6 knit
Round 7 *k2, ssk, k4, k2tog, k2, rep from * around: 30 sts
Rounds 8-10 knit
Round 11 *k2, ssk, k2, k2tog, k2, rep from * around: 24 sts
Rounds 12-14 knit
Round 15 *k2, ssk, k2tog, k2, rep from * around: 18 sts
Round 16 knit
Round 17 k4, ssk, k1, ssk, k2tog, k1, k2tog, k4: 14 sts
Round 18 knit

Leaving sts on the needle(s), stuff body.

Round 19 k5, ssk, k2tog, k5: 12 sts
Round 20 knit

Shape crown (short rows)

Round 1 k4, wrap the next st and turn, p8, wrap the next st and turn, k6, wrap the next st and turn, p4, wrap the next st and turn, k2
Round 2 knit, knitting in wraps with their corresponding sts
Round 3 k2tog, k8, ssk: 10 sts
Round 4 knit

Leaving sts on the needle(s), stuff neck and head.

Timeless Toys

Snout (worked in the round)

Round 1 k2tog, k6, ssk: 8 sts
Round 2 knit
Round 3 k2tog, k4, ssk: 6 sts

BO. Stuff snout. Thread the tail through the inside legs of the bound off sts. Pull up and weave through.

Ears (worked flat, make 2)

CO 6.

Row 1 purl
Row 2 k1, ssk, k2tog, k1: 4 sts
Row 3 purl
Row 4 ssk, k2tog: 2 sts
Row 5 purl

BO. Repeat for second ear.

Tail (worked in I-cord)

CO 2. Work in 2-st I-cord until ~2" long. BO, leaving a 6" tail. Use a running stitch with the yarn tail to weave over and under the "bars" between rows, sewing from the top of the I-cord to the CO edge. Pulling up on this yarn will encourage the tail to curl. Tie off.

Legs and feet (worked in the round, make 4)

CO 6. Join in a round.

Rounds 1-8 knit
Round 9 k1, [kfb] 4 times, k1: 10 sts
Rounds 10-13 knit
Round 14 k1, [k2tog] 4 times, k1: 6 sts

Break yarn, thread tail through remaining sts, pull up and weave through. Stuff foot, leaving leg unstuffed. With brown, sew a loop from the back of the foot at center, over the toe, and back to center back. Pull up tight and tie off. Repeat for each of three other legs and feet.

Assembly and finishing

Sew ears in place on either side of crown. With brown yarn, make duplicate stitch eyes. Make nostrils on snout end with straight stitches. Sew curly tail to bottom of back. Sew legs to body as shown.

Midnight Sun

Two of my grandchildren were born in Fairbanks, Alaska. This section is a tribute to the time I spent there and to the beautiful song and book by Raffi, **Baby Beluga**. *Gifting any of these toys along with the book would be a splendid way to welcome a new baby.*

Baby Beluga

YARN
Brown Sheep Nature Spun Worsted colors 740 (Snow) and 601 (Pepper)

YARDAGE
White: 75 yds
Black: 1 yd

MEASUREMENTS
Baby Beluga is 11" long.

NOTES
1. Please read the Read Me First chapter, pp. 6-16 before you begin.

INSTRUCTIONS

TAIL
Use JMCO (see Technique 3, p. 12) to CO 48. Work in rounds as follows:

Round 1 *k2tog, k20, ssk, rep from *: 44 sts
Round 2 knit
Round 3 *k2tog, k18, ssk, rep from *: 40 sts
Round 4 knit
Round 5 *k2tog, k16, ssk, rep from *: 36 sts
Round 6 knit
Round 7 *k2tog, k14, ssk, rep from *: 32 sts
Round 8 *k2tog, k12, ssk, rep from *: 28 sts
Round 9 *k2tog, k10, ssk, rep from *: 24 sts
Round 10 *k2tog, k8, ssk, rep from *: 20 sts
Round 11 *k2tog, k6, ssk, rep from *: 16 sts
Round 12 *k2tog, k4, ssk, rep from *: 12 sts

Leaving sts on the needle(s), lightly stuff tail. Using a large straight stitch, wrapped around the midpoint of tail, pull up tightly and tie off to shape tail as shown.

BODY AND HEAD (continued in the round)

Note: Round begins at left side of whale's body.

Rounds 1-4 knit
Round 5 *kfb, k3, rep from * around: 15 sts
Rounds 6-8 knit
Round 9 *kfb, k4, rep from * around: 18 sts
Rounds 10-12 knit
Round 13 *kfb, k5, rep from * around: 21 sts
Rounds 14-16 knit
Round 17 *kfb, k6, rep from * around: 24 sts
Rounds 18-20 knit
Round 21 *kfb, k7, rep from * around: 27 sts
Rounds 22-24 knit
Round 25 *kfb, k8, rep from * around: 30 sts
Rounds 26-28 knit
Round 29 *kfb, k9, rep from * around: 33 sts
Rounds 30-32 knit
Round 33 *kfb, k10, rep from * around: 36 sts
Rounds 34-36 knit
Round 37 *kfb, k11, rep from * around: 39 sts
Rounds 38-40 knit
Round 41 *kfb, k12, rep from * around: 42 sts
Rounds 42-44 knit
Round 45 *kfb, k13, rep from * around: 45 sts
Rounds 46-48 knit
Round 49 *kfb, k14, rep from * around: 48 sts

Leaving sts on the needle(s), lightly stuff body.

Rounds 50-54 knit
Round 55 [k2tog, k2] 6 times, k24: 36 sts
Round 56 [kfb, k2] 6 times, k24: 48 sts
Rounds 57-71 knit
Round 72 *k2tog, k2, rep from * around: 36 sts
Rounds 73-75 knit

Leaving sts on the needle(s), add stuffing.

Round 76 *k2tog, k1, rep from * around: 24 sts
Round 77 knit
Round 78 k2tog around: 12 sts
Round 79 knit
Round 80 k2tog around: 6 sts

Add stuffing as necessary. Break yarn, thread tail through remaining sts, pull up and weave through.

FINS (worked flat, make 2)

CO 7.

Rows 1-20 sl1, k6
Row 21 ssk, k3, k2tog: 5 sts
Row 22 knit
Row 23 ssk, k1, k2tog: 3 sts

BO. Repeat for second fin.

ASSEMBLY AND FINISHING

With black, make satin stitch eyes and blowhole. With white, make two 2-st I-cords, one 1-1/2" long and one 2" long. Sew to face for mouth as shown. Attach fins to sides as shown.

Moose

Yarn
Brown Sheep Nature Spun Worsted colors 124 (Butterscotch), 701 (Stone), and 601 (Pepper)

Yardage
Dark brown, 105 yds
Light brown, 25 yds
Black, 1 yd

Measurements
Moose is 8" tall, seated.

Notes
1. Please read the Read Me First chapter, pp. 6-16 before you begin.

Instructions
With dark brown, work basic bottom, p.11, through round 10: 48 sts

Body (continue working in the round)

Rounds 1-24 knit
Round 25 *k2, ssk, k8, k2tog, k2, rep from * around: 42 sts
Round 26 knit
Round 27 *k2, ssk, k6, k2tog, k2, rep from * around: 36 sts
Round 28 knit
Round 29 *k2, ssk, k4, k2tog, k2, rep from * around: 30 sts
Round 30 knit
Round 31 *k2, ssk, k2, k2tog, k2, rep from * around: 24 sts

Leaving sts on the needle(s), lightly stuff body.

Rounds 32-33 knit
Round 34 k6, [k2tog] 6 times, k6: 18 sts
Rounds 35-37 knit

Back neck (worked flat over 14 sts at center back; round begins at center of these sts)

Knit the first 7 sts of the next round. Turn.

Row 1 sl1, p13
Row 2 sl1, k13

Repeat rows 1 and 2 a total of 7 times (14 rows total).

Shape Crown (short rows)

Row 1 p8, p2tog, p1, turn
Row 2 sl1, k3, ssk, k1, turn
Row 3 sl1, p4, p2tog, p1, turn
Row 4 sl1, k5, ssk, k1, turn
Row 5 sl1, p6, p2tog, p1, turn
Row 6 k7, ssk

Eight (8) sts remain in crown.

Leaving sts on the needle(s), lightly stuff neck and head.

From the RS, pick up and knit 9 sts along left side of back neck, knit across 4 sts at center front, pick up and knit 9 sts along right side of back neck, k4 sts from crown. Round (30 sts) now begins at center crown.

Face (worked in the round)

Round 1 knit
Round 2 ssk, k8, k2tog, k6, ssk, k8, k2tog: 26 sts
Round 3 knit
Round 4 ssk, k6, k2tog, k6, ssk, k6, k2tog: 22 sts
Round 5 knit
Round 6 k3, [k2tog] 3 times, k4, [k2tog] 3 times, k3: 16 sts
Rounds 7-18 knit
Round 19 k4, [kfb] twice, k4, [kfb] twice, k4: 20 sts
Rounds 20-22 knit
Round 23 k4, [k2tog] twice, k4, [k2tog] twice, k4: 16 sts

Leaving sts on the needle(s), lightly stuff face.

Round 24 k2tog around: 8 sts

Break yarn, thread tail through remaining sts, pull up and weave through.

Rack of Antlers (worked in the round, make 2)

With light brown, use JMCO (see Technique 3, p. 12), to CO 22.

Round 1 *kfb, k8, kfb, k1, rep from *: 26 sts
Round 2 knit
Round 3 *kfb, k10, kfb, k1, rep from *: 30 sts
Round 4 knit
Round 5 *kfb, k12, kfb, k1, rep from *: 34 sts
Round 6 knit

Leaving sts on the needle(s), very lightly stuff (should be flattish, not roundish).

Antler #1: Slip first 5 sts of the round onto a needle or needle point; slip the last 5 sts of the round onto a second needle or needle point (to be worked in the round). Work as follows:

Round 1 knit
Round 2 *ssk, k1, k2tog, rep from *: 6 sts
Round 3 knit
Round 4 [cdd] twice: 2 sts

BO. Gently stuff this antler.

Antler #2: Slip the next 6 sts from the front of the round onto a needle or needle point; slip the next 6 sts from the end of the round onto a second needle or needle point (to be worked in the round). Work as follows:

Round 1 knit
Round 2 *ssk, k2, k2tog, rep from *: 8 sts
Round 3 knit
Round 4 *ssk, k2tog, rep from *: 4 sts

Round 5 knit
Round 6 [k2tog] twice: 2 sts

BO. Gently stuff this antler.

Antler #3: Twelve (12) sts remain from the original round. Finish them as for antler #2 above.

Use tails to close gaps between antlers. Repeat for second rack.

Tail (twisted cord)

Break off ~12" of light brown yarn. Tie into a circle with an overhand knot. Make a short twisted cord (see Technique 8, p. 12). Tie off and trim.

Ears (worked flat, make 2)

CO 3.

Row 1 purl
Row 2 k1, M1R, k1, M1L, k1: 5 sts
Row 3 purl
Row 4 knit
Row 5 purl
Row 6 ssk, k1, k2tog: 3 sts
Row 7 purl
Row 8 cdd: 1 st

BO. Repeat for second ear.

Front legs and feet (worked in the round, make 2)

CO 9. Join in a round.

Rounds 1-21 knit
Round 22 k2, [kfb] 5 times, k2: 14 sts
Rounds 23-26 knit
Round 27 k2, [k2tog] 5 times, k2: 9 sts
Round 28 *k2tog, k1, rep from * around: 6 sts

Break yarn, thread tail through remaining sts, pull up and weave through. Stuff just the foot, leaving leg unstuffed.

Back legs and feet (worked in the round, make 2)

CO 12. Join in a round.

Rounds 1-25 knit
Round 26 k3, [kfb] 6 times, k3: 18 sts
Rounds 27-30 knit
Round 31 k3, [k2tog] 6 times, k3: 12 sts
Round 32 k2tog around: 6 sts

Break yarn, thread tail through remaining sts, pull up, and weave through. Stuff just the foot, leaving leg unstuffed.

Assembly and finishing

Sew ears and antlers to head as shown. With black, make satin stitch eyes and nostrils, and a straight stitch mouth. Sew legs to front of body as shown. Sew tail to bottom of back.

Polar Bear

YARN
Brown Sheep Nature Spun Worsted colors 730 (Natural) and 601 (Pepper)

YARDAGE
Natural, 105 yds
Black, 2 yds

MEASUREMENTS
Polar bear is 7" tall, seated.

NOTES
1. Please read the Read Me First chapter, pp. 6-16 before you begin.

INSTRUCTIONS
Work basic bottom, p. 11, through round 15: 60 sts.

BODY (continue working in the round)

Rounds 1-8 knit
Round 9 *k2, ssk, k12, k2tog, k2, rep from * around: 54 sts
Rounds 10-14 knit
Round 15 *k2, ssk, k10, k2tog, k2, rep from * around: 48 sts
Rounds 16-20 knit
Round 21 *k2, ssk, k8, k2tog, k2, rep from * around: 42 sts
Rounds 22-26 knit
Round 27 *k2, ssk, k6, k2tog, k2, rep from * around: 36 sts
Round 28 knit
Round 29 *k2, ssk, k4, k2tog, k2, rep from * around: 30 sts
Round 30 knit
Round 31 *k2, ssk, k2, k2tog, k2, rep from * around: 24 sts
Round 32 knit

Leaving sts on the needle(s), stuff body.

BACK NECK (worked flat over 12 sts at center back)

Row 1 k6, turn
Row 2 p12, turn
Row 3 sl1, [kfb, k1] 5 times, k1: 17 sts
Row 4 sl1, p16
Row 5 sl1, k16

Rep rows 4 and 5 six times more.

SHAPE CROWN (short rows)

Row 1 p10, p2tog, p1, turn
Row 2 sl1, k4, ssk, k1, turn
Row 3 sl1, p5, p2tog, p1, turn
Row 4 sl1, k6, ssk, k1, turn
Row 5 sl1, p7, p2tog, p1, turn
Row 6 k9, ssk, k1

Eleven (11) sts remain in crown.

Leaving sts on the needle(s), stuff neck and head.

From the RS, pick up and knit 8 sts along the left side of back neck, [k2tog] 6 times, pick up and knit 9 sts along the right side of back neck, k5 sts from crown. Round (34 sts) now begins at center crown.

FACE (worked in the round)

Round 1 k14, [k2tog] 3 times, k14: 31 sts
Round 2 k5, ssk, k5, k2tog, k3, ssk, k5, k2tog, k5: 27 sts
Round 3 knit
Round 4 k5, ssk, k3, k2tog, k3, ssk, k3, k2tog, k5: 23 sts
Round 5 knit
Round 6 k2tog, k3, ssk, k1, k2tog, k3, ssk, k1, k2tog, k3, ssk: 17 sts
Round 7 knit

Leaving sts on the needle(s), stuff face.

Round 8 k2tog, k3, k2tog, k3, ssk, k3, ssk: 13 sts
Rounds 9-11 knit
Round 12 [k2tog] 3 times, k1, [k2tog] 3 times: 7 sts

Add stuffing to nose as needed. Break yarn, thread tail through remaining sts, pull up and weave through.

EARS (worked flat, make 2)

CO 4.

Row 1 purl
Row 2 knit
Row 3 purl
Row 4 ssk, k2tog: 2 sts

BO. Repeat for second ear.

TAIL (worked flat)

CO 6.

Row 1 purl
Row 2 knit
Row 3 purl
Row 4 knit
Row 5 purl
Row 6 k2tog across: 3 sts
Row 7 p2tog, p1: 2 sts

BO.

LEGS AND FEET (worked in the round, make 4)

CO 12. Join in a round.

Rounds 1-20 knit
Round 21 k3, [kfb] 6 times, k3: 18 sts
Rounds 22-27 knit
Round 28 k3, [k2tog] 6 times, k3: 12 sts
Round 29 k2tog around: 6 sts

Break yarn, thread tail through remaining sts, pull up and weave through. Stuff foot, leaving leg unstuffed. Repeat for three other legs and feet.

ASSEMBLY AND FINISHING

Sew ears in place on either side of crown. With black, make satin stitch eyes and nose as shown. Sew tail to bottom of back. Sew legs to body as shown.

Puffin

Yarn
Brown Sheep Nature Spun Worsted colors N54 (Orange You Glad), 730 (Natural), and 601 (Pepper)

Yardage
White, 45 yds
Black, 35 yds
Orange, 20 yds

Measurements
Puffin is 6-1/2" tall.

Notes
1. Please read the Read Me First chapter, pp. 6-16 before you begin.

Instructions
With white, work large bird bottom, p.11: 52 sts

Body (continue working in the round)

Round 1 knit
Round 2 k2tog, k48, ssk: 50 sts
Round 3 knit
Round 4 k2tog, k46, ssk: 48 sts
Round 5 knit
Round 6 k2tog, k44, ssk: 46 sts
Round 7 knit
Round 8 k2tog, k42, ssk: 44 sts
Round 9 knit
Round 10 k2tog, k40, ssk: 42 sts
Rounds 11-18 knit
Round 19 *k2, ssk, k6, k2tog, k2, rep from * around: 36 sts

Switch to black yarn.

Round 20 knit
Round 21 *k2, ssk, k4, k2tog, k2, rep from * around: 30 sts.
Round 22 knit
Round 23 *k2, ssk, k2, k2tog, k2, rep from * around: 24 sts
Round 24 knit

Leaving sts on the needle(s), lightly stuff body.

Round 25 *k2, ssk, k2tog, k2, rep from * around: 18 sts
Rounds 26-27 knit

Switch to white yarn.

Round 28 knit

HEAD (continued in the round with white)

Round 1 *kfb, k2, rep from * around: 24 sts
Round 2 knit
Round 3 *kfb, k1, rep from * around: 36 sts
Rounds 4-11 knit
Round 12 *k2tog, k1: 24 sts
Round 13 knit

Leaving sts on the needle(s), lightly stuff neck and head.

Round 14 k2tog around: 12 sts
Round 15 knit
Round 16 k2tog around: 6 sts

Add stuffing as necessary. Break yarn, thread tail through remaining sts, pull up and weave through.

WINGS (worked in the round, make only 1)

With black, CO 6. Join in a round.

Round 1 kfb around: 12 sts
Round 2 (and all even-numbered rounds) knit
Round 3 kfb around: 24 sts
Round 5 *kfb, k1, rep from * around: 36 sts
Round 7 *kfb, k2, rep from * around: 48 sts
Round 9 *kfb, k3, rep from * around: 60 sts
Round 11 *kfb, k4, rep from * around: 72 sts
Round 13 *kfb, k5, rep from * around: 84 sts

BO.

CREST (worked flat)

With black, CO 18.

Row 1 (and all WS rows) purl
Row 2 ssk, k14, k2tog: 16 sts
Row 4 ssk, k12, k2tog: 14 sts
Row 6 ssk, k10, k2tog: 12 sts
Row 8 ssk, k8, k2tog: 10 sts
Row 10 ssk, k6, k2tog: 8 sts
Row 12 ssk, k4, k2tog: 6 sts
Rows 14, 16, 18 knit
Row 20 ssk, k2tog: 2 sts

BO.

BEAK (worked in the round)

With orange, CO 20. Join in a round.

Rounds 1-5 knit
Round 6 k2tog, k16, ssk: 18 sts
Round 7 knit
Round 8 *k2tog, k5, ssk, rep from * : 14 sts
Round 9 knit
Round 10 *k2tog, k3, ssk, rep from *: 10 sts
Round 11 knit
Round 12 *k2tog, k1, ssk, rep from *: 6 sts
Round 13 knit
Round 14 [cdd] twice: 2 sts

BO.

FEET AND LEGS (make 2)

Foot:

With orange, CO 25.

Row 1 k11, cdd, k11: 23 sts
Row 2 k11, p1, k11
Row 3 k10, cdd, k10: 21 sts
Row 4 k10, p1, k10
Row 5 k9, cdd, k9: 19 sts
Row 6 k9, p1, k9
Row 7 k8, cdd, k8: 17 sts
Row 8 k8, p1, k8
Row 9 k7, cdd, k7: 15 sts
Row 10 k7, p1, k7
Row 11 k6, cdd, k6: 13 sts
Row 12 k6, p1, k6
Row 13 k5, cdd, k5: 11 sts
Row 14 k5, p1, k5
Row 15 k4, cdd, k4: 9 sts
Row 16 k4, p1, k4
Row 17 k3, cdd, k3: 7 sts
Row 18 k3, p1, k3
Row 19 k2, cdd, k2: 5 sts
Row 20 k2, p1, k2
Row 21 k1, cdd, k1: 3 sts
Row 22 pfb across: 6 sts

Leg: Join in a round by slipping the first st (the one with working yarn attached) onto the needle with the last st. Then pull the last st over the first st onto the right-hand needle. (The first st in the round has traded positions with the last st in the round.) Turn. Work in rounds as follows:

Round 1 kfb around: 12 sts
Rounds 2-3 knit
Round 4 k2tog around: 6 sts

Add a small bit of stuffing. Break yarn, thread tail through remaining sts and pull up. Use this tail to sew the leg (ball) over the back of the foot.

Repeat for second foot.

ASSEMBLY AND FINISHING

Sew the wings (circle) to the center back as shown. Sew the crest to the head as shown. Sew beak to the front of the face. Use white and black yarns and straight stitches to add markings to the beak as shown. Use black and orange yarns and straight stitches and French knots to make eyes as shown. Sew feet to the bottom.

Timeless Toys

Walrus

Yarn
Brown Sheep Nature Spun Worsted colors 148 (Autumn Leaves), 730 (Natural), and 601 (Pepper)

Yardage
Brown, 85 yds
White, 3 yds
Black, 1 yd

Measurements
Walrus is 11" long.

Notes
1. Please read the Read Me First chapter, pp. 6-16 before you begin.

Instructions

Body
Starting at tail, use JMCO (see Technique 3, p. 12) to CO 12. Round begins and ends at the left side of tail. Work in rounds as follows:

Rounds 1-3 knit
Round 4 *kfb, k1, rep from * around: 18 sts
Rounds 5-10 knit
Round 11 *kfb, k2, rep from * around: 24 sts
Rounds 12-17 knit
Round 18 *kfb, k3, rep from * around: 30 sts
Rounds 19-24 knit
Round 25 *kfb, k4, rep from * around: 36 sts
Rounds 26-31 knit
Round 32 *kfb, k5, rep from * around: 42 sts
Rounds 33-38 knit
Round 39 *kfb, k6, rep from * around: 48 sts
Round 40 k23, wrap the next st and turn; sl1, p22, wrap the next st and turn
Round 41 sl1, k22, knit in the wrap with the next st, k24 (to end of round)
Round 42 knit wrap with the first st, k22, wrap the next st and turn; sl1, p22, wrap the next st and turn
Rounds 43-50 rep rounds 41 and 42 four times more

Round 51 knit the first st with its wrap, k47
Round 52 *kfb, k7, rep from * around: 54 sts
Rounds 53-58 knit

Leaving sts on the needle(s), stuff body.

Round 59 k27 (round now begins and ends at this center back)
Round 60 *k2, ssk, k10, k2tog, k2, rep from * around: 48 sts
Rounds 61-63 knit
Round 64 *k2, ssk, k8, k2tog, k2, rep from * around: 42 sts
Rounds 65-67 knit
Round 68 *k2, ssk, k6, k2tog, k2, rep from * around: 36 sts
Rounds 69-71 knit
Round 72 *k2, ssk, k4, k2tog, k2, rep from * around: 30 sts
Rounds 73-79 knit

Leaving sts on the needle(s), stuff remainder of body.

HEAD (short rows)

Row 1 k7, wrap the next st and turn
Row 2 p14, wrap the next st and turn
Row 3 k12, wrap the next st and turn
Row 4 p10, wrap the next st and turn
Row 5 k8, wrap the next st and turn
Row 6 p3 (to center)

FACE (worked in the round)

Round 1 k8 (knitting 3 wraps in with their corresponding sts), [k2tog] 7 times, k8 (knitting 3 wraps in with their corresponding sts): 23 sts
Round 2 k1, k2tog, k6, ssk, k1, k2tog, k6, ssk, k1: 19 sts
Round 3 knit
Round 4 k1, k2tog, k13, ssk, k1: 17 sts
Rounds 5-7 knit

Leaving sts on the needle(s), stuff head and face.

Round 8 [k2tog] 4 times, k1, [k2tog] 4 times: 9 sts

Add stuffing as necessary. Break yarn, thread tail through remaining sts, pull up and weave through.

CHEEKS (worked in the round, make 2)

CO 6. Join in a round.

Round 1 kfb around: 12 sts
Round 2 knit
Round 3 k2tog around: 6 sts

Add a tiny bit of stuffing. Break yarn, thread tail through remaining sts, pull up and weave through. Repeat for second cheek.

Tusks (worked as I-cord, make 2)

With white, CO 3. Work in 3-st I-cord for 8 rows. Last row: k2tog, k1, BO. Repeat for second tusk.

Front flippers (worked in the round, make a right and a left)

Right flipper:

CO 18. Join in a round.

Rounds 1-6 knit
Round 7 k2tog, k14, ssk: 16 sts
Rounds 8-20 knit
Round 21 k2tog, k12, ssk: 14 sts
Rounds 22-24 knit
Round 25 k5, ssk, k2tog, k5: 12 sts
Round 26 knit
Round 27 k4, ssk, k2tog, k4: 10 sts
Round 28 knit
Round 29 k3, ssk, k2tog, k3: 8 sts
Round 30 *k2tog, ssk, rep from *: 4 sts
Round 31 k2tog, k2tog tbl: 2 sts

BO.

Left flipper:

CO 18. Join in a round.

Rounds 1-6 knit
Round 7 k7, ssk, k2tog, k7: 16 sts
Rounds 8-20 knit
Round 21 k6, ssk, k2tog, k6: 14 sts
Rounds 22-24 knit
Round 25 k2tog, k10, ssk: 12 sts
Round 26 knit
Round 27 k2tog, k8, ssk: 10 sts
Round 28 knit
Round 29 k2tog, k6, ssk: 8 sts
Round 30 *ssk, k2tog, rep from *: 4 sts
Round 31 ssk, k2tog: 2 sts

BO.

For each flipper: Put a little stuffing in the tip of the flipper. Fold the tip up before stuffing the rest of the flipper. This will allow for the flipper to bend so the Walrus can "stand."

Assembly and finishing

Use CO tail and running stitch to delineate hind legs as shown. Sew cheeks to front of face as shown. Use black to make satin stitch nose and French knot eyes. Sew a tusk under each cheek. Sew flippers to sides as shown.

Reef

Under the sea is a magical place. What child doesn't experience a fascination with this hidden world at one time or another?

Blue Tang

Yarn

Brown Sheep Cotton Fleece
colors CW765 (Blue Paradise), CW844 (Celery Leaves), CW100 (Cotton Ball), and CW005 (Cavern)

Yardage

Blue, 50 yds
Neon yellow, 20 yds
White, 3 yds
Black, 1 yd

Measurements

Blue tang is 8″ long.

Notes

1. Please read the Read Me First chapter, pp. 6-16 before you begin.

2. Use a smaller needle size with this yarn. Model was knit with US size 4 (3.5 mm) needles.

Instructions

Body (worked in the round)

With blue, use JMCO (see Technique 3, p. 12) to CO 12. Join in a round. (Note: Round begins and ends at the bottom of the fish.)

Rounds 1-2 knit
Round 3 *k1, kfb, k1, kfb, k2, rep from *: 16 sts
Round 4 knit
Round 5 *k1, kfb, k3, kfb, k2, rep from *: 20 sts
Round 6 knit
Round 7 *k1, kfb, k5, kfb, k2, rep from *: 24 sts
Round 8 knit
Round 9 *k1, kfb, k7, kfb, k2, rep from *: 28 sts
Round 10 knit
Round 11 *k1, kfb, k9, kfb, k2, rep from *: 32 sts
Round 12 knit
Round 13 *k1, kfb, k11, kfb, k2, rep from *: 36 sts
Rounds 14-15 knit
Round 16 *k1, kfb, k13, kfb, k2, rep from *: 40 sts
Rounds 17-18 knit
Round 19 *k1, kfb, k15, kfb, k2, rep from *: 44 sts
Rounds 20-21 knit
Round 22 *k1, kfb, k17, kfb, k2, rep from *: 48 sts
Rounds 23-45 knit
Round 46 k21, k2tog, k2, ssk, k21: 46 sts
Round 47 *k1, ssk, k17, k2tog, k1, rep from *: 42 sts

Round 48 k18, k2tog, k2, ssk, k18: 40 sts

Leaving sts on the needle(s), lightly stuff body.

Round 49 *k1, ssk, k14, k2tog, k1, rep from *: 36 sts
Round 50 k15, k2tog, k2, ssk, k15: 34 sts
Round 51 *k1, ssk, k11, k2tog, k1, rep from *: 30 sts
Round 52 k12, k2tog, k2, ssk, k12: 28 sts

Leaving sts on the needle(s), add stuffing.

Round 53 *k1, ssk, k8, k2tog, k1, rep from *: 24 sts
Round 54 k9, k2tog, k2, ssk, k9: 22 sts
Round 55 *k1, ssk, k5, k2tog, k1, rep from *: 18 sts

Leaving sts on the needle(s), add stuffing.

Round 56 k6, k2tog, k2, ssk, k6: 16 sts
Round 57 *k1, ssk, k2, k2tog, k1, rep from *: 12 sts
Round 58 k2tog around: 6 sts

Leaving sts on the needle(s), add stuffing if necessary.

Break yarn, thread tail through remaining sts, pull up and weave through.

CAUDAL FIN (tail, worked in the round)

With yellow, use JMCO to CO 34.

Rounds 1-2 *k1, [p3, k1] 4 times, rep from *
Round 3 *k1, [p2tog, p1, k1] 4 times, rep from *: 26 sts
Rounds 4-6 *k1, [p2, k1] 4 times, rep from *
Round 7 *k1, [p2tog, k1] 4 times, rep from *: 18 sts
Rounds 8-11 *k1, [p1, k1] 4 times, rep from *
Round 12 *[k2tog] 4 times while binding off, k1, BO, rep from *

PECTORAL FINS (worked flat, make 2)

With blue, CO 5.

Row 1 k1, *p1, k1, rep from *
Row 2 p1, *k1, p1, rep from *
Row 3 k1, *pfb, k1, rep from *: 7 sts
Row 4 p1, *k2, p1, rep from *
Row 5 k1, *p2, k1, rep from *
Row 6 rep row 4
Row 7 rep row 5
Row 8 rep row 4

BO.

Repeat for second pectoral fin.

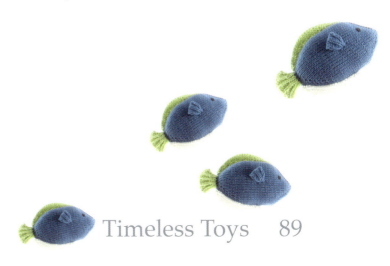

DORSAL FIN (worked flat, in garter st)

With yellow, CO 28.

Row 1 k22, wrap the next st and turn
Row 2 k20, wrap the next st and turn
Row 3 k18, wrap the next st and turn
Row 4 k14, wrap the next st and turn
Row 5 k13, wrap the next st and turn
Row 6 k10, wrap the next st and turn
Row 7 k9, wrap the next st and turn
Row 8 k5, wrap the next st and turn
Row 9 knit to the end, knitting in wraps with their corresponding sts
Row 10 knit, binding off and knitting in wraps with their corresponding sts

ANAL FIN (worked flat, in garter st)

With white, CO 24.

Row 1 k20, wrap the next st and turn
Row 2 k18, wrap the next st and turn
Row 3 k14, wrap the next st and turn
Row 4 k13, wrap the next st and turn
Row 5 k10, wrap the next st and turn
Row 6 k9, wrap the next st and turn
Row 7 knit to the end, knitting in wraps with their corresponding sts
Row 8 knit, binding off and knitting in wraps with their corresponding sts

ASSEMBLY AND FINISHING

Sew fins to body as shown. With black, make satin stitch eyes as shown.

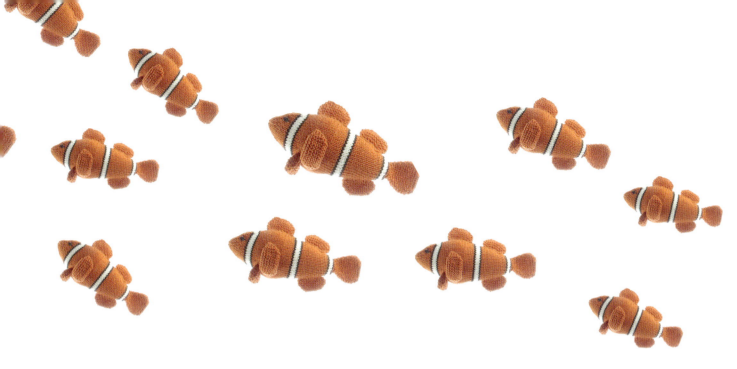

Clown Fish

Yarn
Brown Sheep Cotton Fleece colors CW310 (Wild Orange), CW100 (Cotton Ball), and CW005 (Cavern)

Yardage
Orange, 70 yds
White, 18 yds
Black, 7 yds

Measurements
Clown fish is 10-1/2" long.

Notes
1. Please read the Read Me First chapter, pp. 6-16 before you begin.

2. Use a smaller needle size with this yarn. Model was knit with US size 4 (3.5 mm) needles.

Instructions

Body (worked in the round)

Beginning at tail end of body, with orange, use JMCO (see Technique 3, p. 12) to CO 12. Join in a round. (Note: Round begins and ends at the bottom of the fish.)

Round 1 knit
Round 2 *kfb, k3, kfb, k1, rep from *: 16 sts
Round 3 (with black) knit
Rounds 4-5 (with white) knit
Round 6 (with white) *kfb, k5, kfb, k1, rep from *: 20 sts
Round 7 (with black) knit
Rounds 8-9 (continue with orange) knit
Round 10 *kfb, k7, kfb, k1, rep from *: 24 sts
Rounds 11-13 knit
Round 14 *kfb, k9, kfb, k1, rep from *: 28 sts

Rounds 15-17 knit
Round 18 *kfb, k11, kfb, k1, rep from *: 32 sts
Rounds 19-21 knit
Round 22 *kfb, k13, kfb, k1, rep from *: 36 sts
Rounds 23-25 knit
Round 26 *kfb, k15, kfb, k1, rep from *: 40 sts
Round 27 (with black) knit
Rounds 28-29 (with white) knit
Round 30 (with white) *kfb, k17, kfb, k1, rep from *: 44 sts
Round 31 (with black) knit
Rounds 32-33 (continue with orange) knit
Round 34 *kfb, k19, kfb, k1, rep from *: 48 sts
Rounds 35-37 knit
Round 38 *kfb, k21, kfb, k1, rep from *: 52 sts
Rounds 39-41 knit
Round 42 *kfb, k23, kfb, k1, rep from *: 56 sts
Rounds 43-45 knit
Round 46 *k1, ssk, k22, k2tog, k1, rep from *: 52 sts
Rounds 47-49 knit
Round 50 *k1, ssk, k20, k2tog, k1, rep from *: 48 sts
Rounds 51-53 knit
Round 54 *k1, ssk, k18, k2tog, k1, rep from *: 44 sts
Round 55 (with black) knit
Round 56 (with white) *k1, ssk, k16, k2tog, k1: 40 sts
Round 57 (with white) knit

Leaving sts on the needle(s), lightly stuff body.

Round 58 (with white) *k1, ssk, k14, k2tog, k1, rep from *: 36 sts
Round 59 (with black) knit
Round 60 (continue with orange) *k1, ssk, k12, k2tog, k1, rep from *: 32 sts
Round 61 knit
Round 62 *k1, ssk, k10, k2tog, k1, rep from *: 28 sts
Round 63 knit
Round 64 *k1, ssk, k8, k2tog, k1, rep from *: 24 sts
Round 65 knit
Round 66 *k1, ssk, k6, k2tog, k1, rep from *: 20 sts
Round 67 knit
Round 68 *k1, ssk, k4, k2tog, k1, rep from *: 16 sts
Round 69 knit
Round 70 *k1, ssk, k2, k2tog, k1, rep from *: 12 sts

Leaving sts on the needle(s), lightly stuff front of body.

Round 71 knit
Round 72 k2tog around: 6 sts

Break yarn, thread tail through remaining sts, pull up and weave through.

CAUDAL FIN (tail, worked flat, in garter st)

With orange, CO 7.

Row 1 sl1, k6
Row 2 sl1, kfb, k3, kfb, k1: 9 sts
Rows 3-5 sl1, k8
Row 6 sl1, kfb, k5, kfb, k1: 11 sts
Rows 7-9 sl1, k10
Row 10 sl1, kfb, k7, kfb, k1: 13 sts
Rows 11-19 sl1, k12
Row 20 sl1, ssk, k7, k2tog, k1: 11 sts
Row 21 sl1, k10

BO, working an ssk in the first 2 sts and a k2tog in the last 2 sts.

FORWARD AND REAR DORSAL FINS AND ANAL FIN (worked flat, make 3)

With orange, CO 9.

Row 1 sl1, *kfb, k1, rep from * across: 13 sts
Rows 2-8 sl1, k12
Row 9 sl1, ssk, k7, k2tog, k1: 11 sts
Row 10 sl1, k10
Row 11 sl1, ssk, k5, k2tog, k1: 9 sts
Row 12 sl1, k8

BO, working an ssk in the first 2 sts and a k2tog in the lasts 2 sts. Repeat for rear dorsal and anal fins.

PECTORAL FINS (worked flat, make 2)

With orange, CO 8.

Row 1 sl1, k7
Row 2 kfb across: 16 sts
Rows 3-12 sl1, k15
Row 13 sl1, ssk, k10, k2tog, k1: 14 sts
Row 14 sl1, k13
Row 15 sl1, ssk, k8, k2tog, k1: 12 sts
Row 16 sl1, k11

BO, working an ssk in the first 2 sts and a k2tog in the lasts 2 sts. Repeat for second pectoral fin.

PELVIC FINS (worked flat, make 2)

With orange, CO 4.

Row 1 sl1, k3
Row 2 sl1, [kfb] 2 times, k1: 6 sts
Rows 3-5 sl1, k5
Row 6 sl1, k1, [kfb] 2 times, k2: 8 sts
Rows 7-9 sl1, k7
Row 10 sl1, k2, [kfb] 2 times, k3: 10 sts
Row 11 sl1, k9
Row 12 sl1, ssk, k4, k2tog, k1: 8 sts
Row 13 sl1, k7
Row 14 sl1, ssk, k2, k2tog, k1: 6 sts
Row 15 sl1, k5

BO, working an ssk in the first 2 sts and a k2tog in the lasts 2 sts. Repeat for second pelvic fin.

ASSEMBLY AND FINISHING

Sew fins to body as shown. With black, make satin stitch eyes as shown.

Timeless Toys   93

Crab

Yarn

Brown Sheep Cotton Fleece colors CW201 (Barn Red), CW625 (Terracotta Canyon), CW100 (Cotton Ball), and CW005 (Cavern)

Yardage

Red, 50 yds
Orange, 5 yds
White, 4 yds
Black, 2 yds

Measurements

Crab is 4-1/2" across shell and 7" from tip of claw to end of hindmost leg.

Notes

1. Please read the Read Me First chapter, pp. 6-16 before you begin.
2. Use a smaller needle size with this yarn. Model was knit with US size 4 (3.5 mm) needles.

Instructions

Upper body (worked in the round)

With red, CO 6. Join in a round.

Round 1 kfb around: 12 sts
Round 2 (and every even-numbered round) knit
Round 3 kfb around: 24 sts
Round 5 *kfb, k2, kfb, rep from * around: 36 sts
Round 7 *kfb, k4, kfb, rep from * around: 48 sts
Round 9 *kfb, k6, kfb, rep from * around: 60 sts
Round 11 *kfb, k8, kfb, rep from * around: 72 sts
Round 13 *kfb, k10, kfb, rep from * around: 84 sts
Round 14 knit

Purl 3 rounds. BO.

Under body (worked in the round)

With orange, CO 6. Join in a round.

Work as for upper body through round 13. BO.

Back legs (worked in the round, make 6)

With red, CO 6. Join in a round.

Rounds 1-12 knit

Leaving stitches on the needle(s), lightly stuff upper leg.

Round 13 k2tog around, onto one needle: 3 sts
Rounds 14-21 work as 3-st I-cord
Round 22 k2tog, k1: 2 sts

BO. Repeat for other five legs.

EYES (worked in the round, make 2)

With red, CO 6. Join in a round.

Rounds 1-7 knit

Leaving stitches on the needle(s), lightly stuff eyestalk.

Switch to white.

Round 8 kfb around: 12 sts
Rounds 9-12 knit
Round 13 k2tog around: 6 sts

Leaving stitches on the needle(s), stuff eyeball. Break yarn, thread tail through remaining sts, pull up and weave through. With black, make a French knot pupil in the center of the eyeball as shown. Repeat for second eye.

FRONT LEGS AND CLAWS (worked in the round, make 2)

With red, CO 6. Join in a round.

Rounds 1-12 knit

Leaving stitches on the needle(s), lightly stuff leg.

Rounds 13-24 knit

Leaving stitches on the needle(s), lightly stuff leg.

Round 25 kfb around: 12 sts
Round 26 k4, *kfb, k1, rep from * around: 16 sts
Rounds 27-36 knit

Leaving stitches on the needle(s), stuff claw base.

Round 37 [k2tog] 2 times, k3, ssk, k2, k2tog, k3: 12 sts
Rounds 38-39 knit
Round 40 k4, ssk, k2, k2tog, k2: 10 sts
Rounds 41-42 knit

Leaving stitches on the needle(s), add stuffing to claw.

Round 43 k3, ssk, k2, k2tog, k1: 8 sts
Round 44 knit
Round 45 k2tog around: 4 sts

Leaving stitches on the needle(s), add stuffing to claw as necessary. Break yarn, thread tail through remaining sts, pull up and weave through. With black, use straight stitches to delineate the small and large parts of the claw as shown.

ASSEMBLY AND FINISHING

Stuff the upper body and sew under body to upper body inside edging. Sew back legs and eyes to under body as shown. Sew claws to front of under body as shown. Fold each front leg at center point and tack in place for bend.

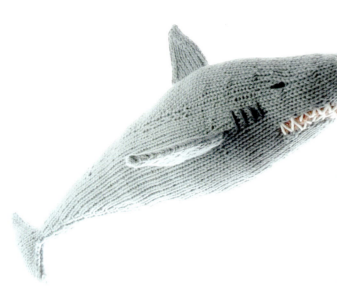

Shark

Yarn

Brown Sheep Cotton Fleece
colors CW375 (Rue), CW625 (Terracotta Canyon), CW100 (Cotton Ball), CW005 (Cavern), and CW385 (Deep Sea Fog)

Yardage

Gray/blue, 125 yds
Orange, 5 yds
White, 3 yds
Black, 1 yd
Blue, 2 yds

Measurements

Shark is 15" long.

Notes

1. Please read the Read Me First chapter, pp. 6-16 before you begin.

2. Use a smaller needle size with this yarn. Model was knit with US size 4 (3.5 mm) needles.

Instructions

Caudal fin (tail, worked in the round)

With gray/blue, use JMCO (see Technique 3, p. 12) to CO 51. Join in a round. (Note: Round begins and ends at the top of the shark.)

Round 1 ssk, k21, k2tog, ssk, k22, k2tog: 47 sts
Round 2 ssk, k19, k2tog, ssk, k20, k2tog: 43 sts
Round 3 ssk, k17, k2tog, ssk, k18, k2tog: 39 sts
Round 4 ssk, k15, k2tog, ssk, k16, k2tog: 35 sts
Round 5 ssk, k13, k2tog, ssk, k14, k2tog: 31 sts
Round 6 ssk, k11, k2tog, ssk, k12, k2tog: 27 sts
Round 7 ssk, k9, k2tog, ssk, k10, k2tog: 23 sts
Round 8 ssk, k7, k2tog, ssk, k8, k2tog: 19 sts
Round 9 ssk, k5, k2tog, ssk, k6, k2tog: 15 sts
Round 10 ssk, k3, k2tog, ssk, k4, k2tog: 11 sts
Round 11 ssk, k3, ssk, k4: 9 sts

Leaving sts on the needle(s), stuff caudal fin.

BODY (continue working in the round)

Rounds 1-4 knit
Round 5 *kfb, k2, rep from * around: 12 sts
Rounds 6-8 knit
Round 9 *kfb, k3, rep from * around: 15 sts
Rounds 10-12 knit
Round 13 *kfb, k4, rep from * around: 18 sts
Rounds 14-16 knit
Round 17 *kfb, k5, rep from * around: 21 sts
Rounds 18-20 knit
Round 21 *kfb, k6, rep from * around: 24 sts
Rounds 22-24 knit
Round 25 *kfb, k7, rep from * around: 27 sts
Rounds 26-28 knit
Round 29 *kfb, k8, rep from * around: 30 sts
Rounds 30-32 knit
Round 33 *kfb, k9, rep from * around: 33 sts
Rounds 34-36 knit
Round 37 *kfb, k10, rep from * around: 36 sts
Rounds 38-40 knit
Round 41 *kfb, k11, rep from * around: 39 sts
Rounds 42-44 knit
Round 45 *kfb, k12, rep from * around: 42 sts
Rounds 46-48 knit
Round 49 *kfb, k13, rep from * around: 45 sts
Rounds 50-52 knit
Round 53 *kfb, k14, rep from * around: 48 sts
Rounds 54-56 knit
Round 57 *kfb, k15, rep from * around: 51 sts
Rounds 58-60 knit
Round 61 *kfb, k16, rep from * around: 54 sts
Rounds 62-64 knit
Round 65 *kfb, k17, rep from * around: 57 sts
Rounds 66-68 knit
Round 69 *kfb, k18, rep from * around: 60 sts

HEAD (continue working in the round)

Rounds 1-6 knit
Round 7 *k2, ssk, k12, k2tog, k2, rep from * around: 54 sts
Rounds 8-13 knit
Round 14 *k2, ssk, k10, k2tog, k2, rep from * around: 48 sts
Rounds 15-20 knit
Round 21 *k2, ssk, k8, k2tog, k2, rep from * around: 42 sts
Rounds 22 knit

Divide for upper and lower jaws: k28, slip the last 14 sts knit onto waste yarn (to reserve for lower jaw), knit across 28 sts for upper jaw, ending on the left side of upper jaw when viewed from the RS.

Nose and mouth (worked flat)

Upper jaw:

Row 1 p28
Row 2 knit
Row 3 purl
Row 4 k5, ssk, k2tog, k10, ssk, k2tog, k5: 24 sts
Rows 5-11 purl WS rows and knit RS rows

CO 14 at the beginning of the next row. Join in a round: 38 sts

Nose: (Note: Round begins at the side of the mouth.)

Round 1 k20, k2tog, k8, ssk, k6: 36 sts
Round 2 ssk, k10, k2tog, k22: 34 sts
Round 3 knit
Round 4 ssk, k8, k2tog, k22: 32 sts
Rounds 5-7 knit
Round 8 ssk, k6, k2tog, k6, ssk, k6, k2tog, k6: 28 sts
Round 9 knit
Round 10 ssk, k4, k2tog, ssk, k2, k2tog, ssk, k4, k2tog, ssk, k2, k2tog: 20 sts
Round 11 knit
Round 12 ssk, k2, k2tog, ssk, k2tog, ssk, k2, k2tog, ssk, k2tog: 12 sts

Use the Kitchener stitch to graft the top 6 sts to the bottom 6 sts of the nose.

Stuff head and nose.

Lower jaw:

Place 14 sts from waste yarn back on the needles.

Row 1 knit
Row 2 purl
Row 3 ssk, k10, k2tog: 12 sts
Rows 4-8 purl WS rows and knit RS rows
Row 9 ssk, k8, k2tog: 10 sts
Row 10 purl
Row 11 ssk, k6, k2tog: 8 sts
Row 12 purl

BO.

From the RS with orange, pick up and knit 24 sts around the lower jaw.

Row 1 p9, [pfb] 2 times, p2, [pfb] 2 times, p9: 28 sts
Row 2 k24, wrap the next st and turn; p21, wrap the next st and turn; knit to end, knitting in wrap with corresponding st
Row 3 p28, purling in wrap with corresponding st

BO.

Dorsal fin (worked in the round)

With blue/gray, use JMCO to CO 20.

Round 1 knit
Round 2 k1, ssk, k14, k2tog, k1: 18 sts
Round 3 knit
Round 4 k1, ssk, k12, k2tog, k1: 16 sts
Round 5 knit
Round 6 k1, ssk, k10, k2tog, k1: 14 sts
Rounds 7-9 knit
Round 10 k4, k2tog, k2, ssk, k4: 12 sts
Round 11 knit
Round 12 k3, k2tog, k2, ssk, k3: 10 sts
Round 13 knit
Round 14 k2, k2tog, k2, ssk, k2: 8 sts
Round 15 knit
Round 16 k1, k2tog, k2, ssk, k1: 6 sts
Round 17 knit
Round 18 k1, k2tog, ssk, k1: 4 sts

Break yarn, thread tail through remaining sts, pull up and weave through. Lightly stuff dorsal fin.

ASSEMBLY AND FINISHING

Sew lower jaw to upper jaw as shown, adding and adjusting stuffing as required. Sew dorsal and pectoral fins to body as shown. With black, make satin stitch eyes as shown. With blue, make duplicate stitch nostrils and straight stitch gills as shown. With white, make straight stitch teeth as shown.

PECTORAL FINS (worked in the round, make 2)

With blue/gray, use JMCO to CO 24.

Round 1 knit
Round 2 k1, ssk, k18, k2tog, k1: 22 sts
Round 3 knit
Round 4 k1, ssk, k16, k2tog, k1: 20 sts
Round 5 knit
Round 6 k1, ssk, k14, k2tog, k1: 18 sts
Rounds 7-9 knit
Round 10 k6, k2tog, k2, ssk, k6: 16 sts
Rounds 11-13 knit
Round 14 k5, k2tog, k2, ssk, k5: 14 sts
Rounds 15-17 knit
Round 18 k4, k2tog, k2, ssk, k4: 12 sts
Rounds 19-21 knit
Round 22 k3, k2tog, k2, ssk, k3: 10 sts
Rounds 23-25 knit
Round 26 k2, k2tog, k2, ssk, k2: 8 sts
Rounds 27-29 knit
Round 30 k1, k2tog, k2, ssk, k1: 6 sts
Rounds 31-33 knit
Round 34 k1, k2tog, ssk, k1: 4 sts

Break yarn, thread tail through remaining sts, pull up and weave through. Lightly stuff pectoral fin. Repeat for second fin.

Starfish

YARN
Brown Sheep Cotton Fleece color CW120 (Honey Butter)

YARDAGE
80 yds

MEASUREMENTS
Starfish is ~5-1/2" from center to end of each arm.

NOTES
1. Please read the Read Me First chapter, pp. 6-16 before you begin.

2. Use a smaller needle size with this yarn. Model was knit with US size 4 (3.5 mm) needles.

3. To prevent holes on either side of bobbles, knit the first st following a MB through the back loop. On the next round, knit the bobble st through the back loop.

INSTRUCTIONS

CENTRAL DISC—TOP (worked in the round)

CO 5. Join in a round.

Round 1 kfb around: 10 sts
Round 2 knit
Round 3 *kfb, k1, rep from * around: 15 sts
Round 4 knit
Round 5 *k1, MB (see Abbreviations, p. 14), k1, rep from * around
Round 6 knit
Round 7 *kfb, k1, kfb, rep from * around: 25 sts
Round 8 knit
Round 9 *k2, MB, k2, rep from * around
Round 10 knit
Round 11 *[kfb] twice, k3, rep from * around: 35 sts
Round 12 knit
Round 13 *k4, MB, k2, rep from * around
Round 14 knit
Round 15 *k2, [kfb] twice, k3, rep from * around: 45 sts
Round 16 knit
Round 17 *k6, MB, k2, rep from * around
Round 18 knit
Round 19 *k4, [kfb] twice, k3, rep from * around: 55 sts

Knit the first 3 sts of the next round. Then slip all sts onto waste yarn to reserve for later.

CENTRAL DISC–BOTTOM (worked in the round)

CO 5. Join in a round.

Round 1 kfb around: 10 sts
Round 2 knit
Round 3 *kfb, k1, rep from * around: 15 sts
Rounds 4-6 knit
Round 7 *[kfb] twice, k1, rep from * around: 25 sts
Rounds 8-10 knit
Round 11 *k1, [kfb] twice, k2, rep from * around: 35 sts
Rounds 12-14 knit
Round 15 *k2, [kfb] twice, k3, rep from * around: 45 sts
Rounds 16-18 knit
Round 19 *k3, [kfb] twice, k4, rep from * around: 55 sts

Slip all sts onto waste yarn to reserve for later.

ARMS (worked in the round, make 5)

Holding central disc sections wrong sides together, slip the first 11 sts from the top disc and the first 11 sts from the bottom disc onto needles. (Note: The bobble should fall in the center of the 11 sts of the top disc.) Join in a round. The round should begin at the left side of the arm when viewed from above, so that the sts in the bottom of the arm are worked first. Leave a 6" to 8" tail when beginning, as this will be used to sew together and neaten the gaps that will form between the arms.

Round 1 knit
Round 2 k16, MB, k5
Round 3 knit
Round 4 k3, ssk, k1, k2tog, k6, ssk, k1, k2tog, k3: 18 sts
Round 5 knit
Round 6 k13, MB, k4
Rounds 7-9 knit
Round 10 rep round 6

Round 11 knit
Round 12 k2, ssk, k1, k2tog, k4, ssk, k1, k2tog, k2: 14 sts
Round 13 knit
Round 14 k10, MB, k3
Rounds 15-17 knit
Round 18 rep round 14
Round 19 knit
Round 20 k1, ssk, k1, k2tog, k2, ssk, k1, k2tog, k1: 10 sts
Round 21 knit
Round 22 k7, MB, k2
Rounds 23-25 knit
Round 26 rep round 21
Round 27 knit
Round 28 ssk, k1, k2tog, ssk, k1, k2tog: 6 sts
Round 29 knit

Break yarn, thread tail through remaining sts, pull up and weave through. Lightly stuff arm.

Work the second, third, and fourth arms as for the first, slipping the next 11 sts from top and bottom of body to needle(s) for each arm.

Before starting the fifth and final arm, lightly stuff the body, pressing the center of the bottom of the body up into the center of the top of the body (making the bottom concave), as shown. Stitch the centers of the body sections together at their centers to maintain this shape.

Complete the fifth arm as for the others, lightly stuffing the arm before each decrease round and before weaving tail through remaining sts.

FINISHING

Use tails to close up and neaten gaps between arms.

Serengeti

This section includes the first toys I ever designed, although they've been updated for this shiny new appearance. They were inspired by photographs I made in Tanzania and Zimbabwe and gifted to my (then) 2- and 3-year-old grandsons.

Elephant

YARN
Brown Sheep Lamb's Pride Worsted colors M03 (Grey Heather) and M175 (Bronze Patina)

YARDAGE
Grey, 120 yds
Brown, 3 yds

MEASUREMENTS
Elephant is 6-1/2″ tall, seated.

NOTES
1. Please read the Read Me First chapter, pp. 6-16 before you begin.

INSTRUCTIONS
Work basic bottom, p. 11, through round 15: 60 sts.

BODY (continue working in the round)

Rounds 1-8 knit
Round 9 *k2, ssk, k12, k2tog, k2, rep from * around: 54 sts
Rounds 10-14 knit
Round 15 *k2, ssk, k10, k2tog, k2, rep from * around: 48 sts
Rounds 16-20 knit
Round 21 *k2, ssk, k8, k2tog, k2, rep from * around: 42 sts
Rounds 22-24 knit
Round 25 *k2, ssk, k6, k2tog, k2, rep from * around: 36 sts

Leaving sts on the needle(s), stuff body.

Round 26 k2tog around: 18 sts

BACK NECK (worked flat over 10 sts at center back; round begins at center of these sts)

Knit the first 5 sts of the next round. Turn. *p1, pfb, rep from * four times more: 15 sts. Turn.

Row 1 sl1, k14
Row 2 sl1, p14

Repeat rows 1 and 2 a total of 6 times, then repeat row 1 once more (13 rows total).

SHAPE CROWN (short rows)

Row 1 sl1, p8, p2tog, p1, turn
Row 2 sl1, k4, ssk, k1, turn
Row 3 sl1, p5, p2tog, p1, turn
Row 4 sl1, k6, ssk, k1, turn
Row 5 sl1, p7, p2tog, turn
Row 6 sl1, k7, ssk

Nine (9) sts remain in crown.

From the RS, pick up and knit 8 sts along left side of neck; knit across 8 sts at center front neck; pick up and knit 8 sts along right side of neck; k2tog, k3 sts from crown. Round (32 sts) now begins at center crown.

FACE (worked in the round)

Round 1 k9, k2tog, k10, ssk, k9: 30 sts
Round 2 knit
Round 3 k8, k2tog, k10, ssk, k8: 28 sts
Round 4 knit
Round 5 k7, k2tog, k10, ssk, k7: 26 sts
Round 6 knit
Round 7 k6, k2tog, k10, ssk, k6: 24 sts

Leaving sts on the needle(s), stuff neck, head, and face.

Round 8 *k1, k2tog, rep from * around: 16 sts
Round 9 knit
Round 10 k2tog, k1, [k2tog] 6 times, k1: 9 sts

Leaving sts on the needle(s), add stuffing as needed. Break yarn, thread tail through remaining sts, pull up and weave through.

TRUNK (worked flat, then in I-cord)

CO 15.

Row 1 purl
Row 2 k6, cdd, k6: 13 sts
Rows 3,5,7 purl
Row 4 k5, cdd, k5: 11 sts
Row 6 k4, cdd, k4: 9 sts
Row 8 k3, cdd, k3: 7 sts

Continue in 7-st I-cord for five rows.

In I-cord: ssk, k3, k2tog: 5 sts

Continue in 5-st I-cord for 15 rows.

BO.

EARS (worked flat, make 2)

CO 9.

Row 1 (and all odd-numbered rows) purl
Row 2 k4, M1R, k1, M1L, k4: 11 sts
Row 4 k5, M1R, k1, M1L, k5: 13 sts
Row 6 k6, M1R, k1, M1L, k6: 15 sts
Row 8 k7, M1R, k1, M1L, k7: 17 sts
Row 10 k8, M1R, k1, M1L, k8: 19 sts
Rows 12,14,16 knit
Row 18 k1, ssk, k13, k2tog, k1: 17 sts
Row 20 k1, ssk, k11, k2tog, k1: 15 sts
Row 22 k1, ssk, k3, cdd, k3, k2tog, k1: 11 sts
Row 24 k1, ssk, k1, cdd, k1, k2tog, k1: 7 sts
Row 26 k1, ssk, k1, k2tog, k1: 5 sts
Row 28 ssk, k1, k2tog: 3 sts

BO. Fold cast-on edge in half and seam together.

Assembly and finishing

Sew the trunk to center of face, lightly stuffing the top (above I-cord). With brown and satin stitch, embroider eyes on either side of the top of the trunk. With the RS of ear inside, and the WS of ear forming the outside of cupped ear, sew one upper edge of ear to the side of the back neck where sts were picked up for face. Repeat for second ear. Sew tail to bottom of back at center. Sew legs to body as shown.

Tail

With one strand of grey and one strand of brown, make a twisted cord (see Technique 8, p. 13) about 1-1/4" long.

Legs and feet (worked in the round, make 4)

CO 15. Join in a round.

Rounds 1-25 knit
Round 26 k4, [kfb] 7 times, k4: 22 sts
Rounds 27-30 knit
Round 31 k4, [k2tog] 7 times, k4: 15 sts
Round 32 knit
Round 33 *k2tog, k1, k2tog, rep from * around: 9 sts

Break yarn, thread tail through remaining sts, pull up and weave through. Stuff foot, leaving leg unstuffed. Repeat for other three legs and feet.

Giraffe

Yarn
Brown Sheep Lamb's Pride Worsted colors M14 (Sunburst Gold) and M89 (Roasted Coffee)

Yardage
Gold, 80 yds
Brown, 8 yds

Measurements
Giraffe is 10" tall, seated.

Notes
1. Please read the Read Me First chapter, pp. 6-16 before you begin.

Instructions
With gold, Work basic bottom, p. 11, through round 10: 48 sts.

Body (continue working in the round)

Rounds 1-10 knit
Round 11 *k2, ssk, k8, k2tog, k2, rep from * around: 42 sts
Rounds 12-16 knit
Round 17 *k2, ssk, k6, k2tog, k2, rep from * around: 36 sts
Rounds 18-22 knit
Round 23 *k2, ssk, k4, k2tog, k2, rep from * around: 30 sts
Rounds 24-26 knit
Round 27 *k2, ssk, k2, k2tog, k2, rep from * around: 24 sts
Round 28 knit

Leaving sts on the needle(s), lightly stuff body.

Round 29 k6, [k2tog] 6 times, k6: 18 sts

NECK (continue working in the round)

Rounds 1-25 knit

Leaving sts on the needle(s), lightly stuff neck.

BACK OF HEAD (worked flat over 12 sts at center back; round begins at center of these sts)

Knit the first 6 sts of the next round, turn.

Row 1 sl1, p11
Row 2 sl1, k11

Repeat rows 1 and 2 a total of 5 times (10 rows total).

SHAPE CROWN (short rows)

Row 1 sl1, p6, p2tog, p1, turn
Row 2 sl1, k3, ssk, k1, turn
Row 3 sl1, p4, p2tog, p1, turn
Row 4 sl1, k5, ssk, k1, turn
Row 5 p6, p2tog, turn
Row 6 k5, ssk

Six (6) sts remain in crown.

From the RS, pick up and knit 7 sts along left side of neck; knit across 6 sts at center front neck; pick up and knit 7 sts along right side of neck; knit 3 sts from crown. Round (26 sts) now begins at center crown.

FACE (worked in the round)

Round 1 k10, ssk, k2, k2tog, k10: 24 sts
Round 2 knit
Round 3 k10, ssk, k2tog, k10: 22 sts
Round 4 knit
Round 5 k2, [k2tog] 4 times, k2, [ssk] 4 times, k2: 14 sts

Rounds 6-8 knit

Leaving sts on the needle(s), lightly stuff head, crown, and face.

Round 9 k2tog, k2, k2tog, k2, ssk, k2, ssk: 10 sts
Rounds 10-11 knit
Round 12 [k2tog] twice, k2, [k2tog] twice: 6 sts

Leaving sts on the needle(s), add stuffing to nose as needed. Break yarn, thread tail through remaining sts, pull up and weave through.

TAIL

Cut 6 pieces of brown about 10" long. Use crochet hook to thread 2 pieces through each of 3 stitches along center back at the bottom of the body (in a vertical row). Divide into three groups of 4 strands each and braid the tail for about 1-1/2". Tie securely and trim fringed ends to about 1/2".

EARS (worked flat in garter stitch, make 2)

With gold, CO 9.

Row 1 knit
Row 2 k1, ssk, k3, k2tog, k1: 7 sts
Row 3 knit
Row 4 k1, ssk, k1, k2tog, k1: 5 sts
Row 5 knit
Row 6 ssk, k1, k2tog: 3 sts
Row 7 knit
Row 8 k2tog, k1: 2 sts

BO. Repeat for second ear.

HORNS (worked as I-cord, make 2)

With brown, CO 2. Work in 2-st I-cord for 8 rows. BO. Repeat for second horn.

LEGS AND FEET (worked in the round, make 4)

With gold, CO 9. Join in a round.

Rounds 1-30 knit
Round 31 k2, [kfb] 5 times, k2: 14 sts
Rounds 32-35 knit
Round 36 k2, [k2tog] 5 times, k2: 9 sts
Round 37 *k2tog, k1, rep from * around: 6 sts

Break yarn, thread tail through remaining sts, pull up and weave through. Stuff foot, leaving leg unstuffed. Repeat for three other legs.

ASSEMBLY AND FINISHING

With brown, using chain stitch, work a "mane" along center back from top of head to just below the point where the neck meets the back. Fold each ear in half and sew to top of head on either side of crown, as shown. Attach horns to crown, as shown. With brown, make French knot eyes on face in front of ears. Sew legs to front of body, as shown.

Lion

Yarn

Brown Sheep Lamb's Pride Worsted colors M115 (Oatmeal), M08 (Wild Oak), and M05 (Onyx)

Yardage

Beige, 50 yds
Brown, 10 yds
Black, 1/2 yd

Measurements

Lion is 7" tall, seated.

Notes

1. Please read the Read Me First chapter, pp. 6-16 before you begin.

Instructions

With beige, work basic bottom, p. 11, through round 10: 48 sts.

Body (continue working in the round)

Rounds 1-10 knit
Round 11 *k2, ssk, k8, k2tog, k2, rep from * around: 42 sts
Rounds 12-18 knit
Round 19 *k2, ssk, k6, k2tog, k2, rep from * around: 36 sts
Rounds 20-24 knit
Round 25 *k2, ssk, k4, k2tog, k2, rep from * around: 30 sts
Rounds 26-30 knit
Round 31 *k2, ssk, k2, k2tog, k2, rep from * around: 24 sts

Leaving sts on the needle(s), stuff body.

Round 32 knit
Round 33 k2tog around: 12 sts

Back neck (worked flat over 6 sts at center back; round begins at center of these sts)

Knit the first 3 sts of the next round. Turn, pfb across: 12 sts. Turn.

Row 1 sl1, k11
Row 2 sl1, p11

Repeat rows 1 and 2 a total of 5 times, then repeat row 1 once more (11 rows total).

SHAPE CROWN (short rows)

Row 1 p7, p2tog, p1, turn
Row 2 sl1, k3, ssk, k1, turn
Row 3 sl1, p4, p2tog, p1, turn
Row 4 sl1, k5, ssk, k1, turn
Row 5 p6, p2tog, turn
Row 6 k5, ssk

Six (6) sts remain in crown.

From the RS, pick up and knit 7 sts along left side of neck; knit across 6 sts at center front neck; pick up and knit 7 sts along right side of neck; knit 3 sts from crown. Round (26 sts) now begins at center crown.

FACE (worked in the round)

Round 1 k10, ssk, k2, k2tog, k10: 24 sts
Round 2 knit
Round 3 k10, ssk, k2tog, k10: 22 sts
Round 4 k3, ssk, k2tog, k8, ssk, k2tog, k3: 18 sts
Round 5 knit
Round 6 k2, ssk, k2tog, k6, ssk, k2tog, k2: 14 sts
Round 7 knit

Leaving sts on the needle(s), stuff neck, head, and face.

Round 8 k1, ssk, k2tog, k4, ssk, k2tog, k1: 10 sts
Round 9 knit

Leaving sts on the needle(s), add stuffing to nose as needed.

Round 10 ssk, k2tog, k2, ssk, k2tog: 6 sts

Break yarn, thread tail through remaining sts, pull up and weave through.

imeless Toys

Ears (worked flat, make 2)

With beige, CO 5.

Row 1 purl
Row 2 knit
Row 3 purl
Row 4 ssk, k1, k2tog: 3 sts
Row 5 purl

BO. Repeat for second ear.

Tail

With beige, work a 3-st I-cord for 30 rows. Switch to brown and continue in I-cord for 2 more rows. BO.

Legs and feet (worked in the round, make 4)

With beige, CO 6. Join in a round.

Rounds 1-24 knit
Round 25 k1, [kfb] 4 times, k1: 10 sts
Rounds 26-29 knit
Round 30 k1, [k2tog] 4 times, k1: 6 sts

Break yarn, thread tail through remaining sts, pull up and weave through. Stuff foot, leaving leg unstuffed. Repeat for three other legs.

Assembly and finishing

Sew ears to crown as shown. Using single strands of brown (about 2-1/2" long) attach fringe around face, ears, and back of head as shown. Then give the mane a "haircut" to about 1/2" long. Use brown and satin stitch (horizontally) to make eyes, using a black straight stitch (vertically) in the center of each, as shown. Sew tail to lower back at center. Sew legs to front of body as shown.

Monkey

Yarn

Brown Sheep Lamb's Pride Worsted colors M02 (Brown Heather), M10 (Creme), M180 (Ruby Red), and M05 (Onyx)

Yardage

Brown, 65 yds
Cream, 15 yds
Red, 1 yd
Black, 1 yd

Measurements

Monkey is 6-1/2" tall, seated.

Notes

1. Please read the Read Me First chapter, pp. 6-16 before you begin.

Instructions

Work basic bottom, p. 11, through round 10: 48 sts.

Body (continue working in the round)

Rounds 1-10 knit
Round 11 *k2, ssk, k8, k2tog, k2, rep from * around: 42 sts
Rounds 12-18 knit
Round 19 *k2, ssk, k6, k2tog, k2, rep from * around: 36 sts
Rounds 20-24 knit
Round 25 *k2, ssk, k4, k2tog, k2, rep from * around: 30 sts
Rounds 26-30 knit
Round 31 *k2, ssk, k2, k2tog, k2, rep from * around: 24 sts

Leaving sts on the needle(s), stuff body.

Round 32 knit
Round 33 k2tog around: 12 sts

Timeless Toys   113

HEAD (continue working in the round)

Round 1 knit
Round 2 kfb around: 24 sts
Rounds 3-4 knit
Round 5 *kfb, k1, rep from * around: 36 sts
Rounds 6-11 knit
Round 12 *k2tog, k1, rep from * around: 24 sts

Leaving sts on the needle(s), lightly stuff neck and head.

Round 13 knit
Round 14 k2tog around: 12 sts

Leaving sts on the needle(s), add stuffing to head as needed.

Round 15 k2tog around: 6 sts

Break yarn, thread tail through remaining sts, pull up and weave through.

MUZZLE (worked in the round, stuffed, and sewn on)

With cream, CO 20. Join in a round.

Rounds 1-3 knit
Round 4 k3, ssk, k2tog, k6, ssk, k2tog, k3: 16 sts
Round 5 k4, stop

Use the Kitchener stitch to graft remaining sts together (8 on the top and 8 on the bottom).

EARS (worked flat, make 2)

With cream, CO 5.

Row 1 purl
Row 2 knit
Row 3 purl
Row 4 k1, cdd, k1: 3 sts

BO. Repeat for second ear. Sew ears in place on sides of head as shown.

TAIL (worked in the round, stuffed as you go)

With brown, CO 6. Join in a round.

Rounds 1-2 knit
Round 3 k4, wrap the next st and turn, p2, wrap the next st and turn, k4, knitting in the wrap with the third of these 4 sts
Round 4 k1, knit in the wrap with the next st, k4
Round 5 knit

Repeat rounds 3-5 eleven times more, periodically adding a light stuffing. The eraser end of a pencil will help with tucking in the stuffing.

End by knitting 36 rounds even, stuffing as you go. BO.

ARMS (worked in the round, make 2)

With brown, CO 6. Join in a round.

Rounds 1-25 knit

Switch to cream.

Round 26 knit
Round 27 k2, [kfb] twice, k2: 8 sts
Rounds 28-31 knit
Round 32 k2, [k2tog] twice, k2: 6 sts

Break yarn, thread tail through remaining sts, pull up and weave through. Stuff only the cream portion (hand). Repeat for second arm.

LEGS (worked in the round, make 2)

With brown, CO 8. Join in a round.

Rounds 1-30 knit

Switch to cream.

Round 31 knit
Round 32 k2, [kfb] 4 times, k2: 12 sts
Rounds 33-36 knit
Round 37 k2, [k2tog] 4 times, k2: 8 sts
Round 38 k2tog, k4, k2tog: 6 sts

Break yarn, thread tail through remaining sts, pull up and weave through. Stuff only the cream portion (foot). Repeat for second leg.

ASSEMBLY AND FINISHING

Lightly stuff muzzle and sew to face as shown. Use red and backstitch embroidery to make the lip line. With black, embroider satin stitch eyes as shown. Sew base of tail to center of lower back, with the BO edge pointing down. Sew sides of tail to back for ~3/4" up from base. Sew arms and legs to body as shown.

Timeless Toys 115

Zebra

Yarn
Brown Sheep Lamb's Pride Worsted colors M10 (Creme) and M05 (Onyx)

Yardage
White, 50 yds
Black, 70 yds

Measurements
Zebra is 6-1/2" tall, seated.

Notes
1. Please read the Read Me First chapter, pp. 6-16 before you begin.

2. Alternate 2 rounds of black with 2 rounds of white throughout, except where specifically directed otherwise.

Instructions
Work basic bottom, p. 11, through round 10: 48 sts.

Body (continue working in the round)

Rounds 1-10 knit
Round 11 *k2, ssk, k8, k2tog, k2, rep from * around: 42 sts
Rounds 12-17 knit
Round 18 *k2, ssk, k6, k2tog, k2, rep from * around: 36 sts
Rounds 19-23 knit
Round 24 *k2, ssk, k4, k2tog, k2, rep from * around: 30 sts
Rounds 25-28 knit
Round 29 *k2, ssk, k2, k2tog, k2, rep from * around: 24 sts
Round 30 knit

Leaving sts on the needle(s), stuff body.

Round 31 k2tog around: 12 sts

Back neck (worked flat over 6 sts at center back; round begins at center of these sts)

Knit the first 3 sts of the next round, with white. Turn, pfb across, with white: 12 sts. Turn. Continue alternating 2 rows of black with 2 rows of white.

Row 1 sl1, k11
Row 2 sl1, p11

Repeat rows 1 and 2 a total of 6 times, then repeat row 1 once more (13 rows total).

SHAPE CROWN (short rows, continue striping)

Row 1 p7, p2tog, p1, turn
Row 2 sl1, k3, ssk, k1, turn
Row 3 sl1, p4, p2tog, p1, turn
Row 4 sl1, k5, ssk, k1, turn
Row 5 p6, p2tog, turn
Row 6 k5, ssk

Six (6) sts remain in crown.

With white, from the RS, pick up and knit 8 sts along left side of neck; knit across 6 sts at center front neck; pick up and knit 8 sts along right side of neck; knit 3 sts from crown. Round (28 sts) now begins at center crown.

FACE (worked in the round; continue striping through round 9)

Round 1 k11, ssk, k2, k2tog, k11: 26 sts
Round 2 knit
Round 3 k11, ssk, k2tog, k11: 24 sts
Round 4 knit
Round 5 k3, [ssk] 4 times, k2, [k2tog] 4 times, k3: 16 sts
Rounds 6-8 knit

Leaving sts on the needle(s), stuff neck, head, and face.

Round 9 k1, ssk, k2, ssk, [k2, k2tog] twice, k1: 12 sts

Complete with white:

Rounds 10-11 knit
Round 12 k2tog around: 6 sts
Rounds 13-14 knit

Leaving sts on the needle(s), add stuffing to nose as needed. Break yarn, thread tail through remaining sts, pull up and weave through.

TAIL

Cut 6 pieces of black about 10" long. Use crochet hook to thread 2 pieces through each of 3 stitches along center back at the bottom of the body (in a vertical row). Divide into three groups of 4 strands each and braid the tail for about 1-1/2". Tie securely and trim fringed ends to about 1/2".

EARS (worked flat, make 2)

With black, CO 9.

Row 1 knit
Row 2 k1, ssk, k3, k2tog, k1: 7 sts
Row 3 knit
Row 4 k1, ssk, k1, k2tog, k1: 5 sts
Row 5 knit
Row 6 ssk, k1, k2tog: 3 sts
Row 7 knit
Row 8 k2tog, k1: 2 sts

BO. Repeat for second ear.

Timeless Toys

LEGS AND FEET (worked in the round, make 4)

With white, CO 9. Join in a round. Continue alternating 2 rounds of white with 2 rounds of black for 22 rounds. Continue in black:

Round 1 knit
Round 2 k2, [kfb] 5 times, k2: 14 sts
Rounds 3-6 knit
Round 7 k2, [k2tog] 5 times, k2: 9 sts
Round 8 *k2tog, k1, rep from * around: 6 sts

Break yarn, thread tail through remaining sts, pull up and weave through. Stuff foot, leaving leg unstuffed. Repeat for three other legs.

ASSEMBLY AND FINISHING

Fold each ear in half and sew to top of head on either side of crown. With black, make French knot eyes on face in front of ears. To make the mane, cut lengths of black and lengths of white (about 6" long). Using double strands and matching the stripe color, attach fringe to center back, beginning between ears. Trim the mane to 3/8". Sew legs to front of body as shown.

Southwest

The Southwest is certainly not without its distinctive collection of critters. These are a few that really tickle me.

Armadillo

Yarn
Brown Sheep Cotton Fleece colors CW135 (Slate Charcoal) and CW005 (Cavern)

Yardage
Grey, 95 yds
Black, 1 yd

Measurements
Armadillo is 15-1/2" long.

Notes
1. Please read the Read Me First chapter, pp. 6-16 before you begin.

2. Use a smaller needle size with this yarn. Model was knit with US size 4 (3.5 mm) needles.

Instructions
Work basic bottom, p. 11, through round 15: 60 sts.

Body (continue working in the round)

Note: Round begins at center belly.

Rounds 1-6 knit

Banding pattern:
Round 7 k10, p40, k10
Rounds 8-9 knit

Rounds 10-30 rep 3-round banding pattern (rounds 7-9) seven times more
Round 31 rep round 7, then k30 to move beginning of round to center back
Rounds 32-34 knit
Round 35 *k2, ssk, k12, k2tog, k2, rep from * around: 54 sts
Rounds 36-37 knit
Round 38 *k2, ssk, k10, k2tog, k2, rep from * around: 48 sts
Rounds 39-40 knit
Round 41 *k2, ssk, k8, k2tog, k2, rep from * around: 42 sts
Rounds 42-43 knit
Round 44 *k2, ssk, k6, k2tog, k2, rep from * around: 36 sts
Round 45 knit

Leaving sts on the needle(s), lightly stuff body.

Head (continue working in the round)

Round 1 k2tog around: 18 sts
Round 2 knit
Round 3 [kfb] 6 times, k6, [kfb] 6 times: 30 sts
Rounds 4-6 knit

SHAPE CROWN (short rows)

Row 1 k8, wrap the next st and turn
Row 2 p16, wrap the next st and turn
Row 3 k14, wrap the next st and turn
Row 4 p12, wrap the next st and turn
Row 5 k10, wrap the next st and turn
Row 6 p8, wrap the next st and turn
Row 7 k4

Finish by knitting one round, knitting in six wraps with their corresponding sts.

FACE (worked in the round)

Round 1 *k3, ssk, k2tog, k3, rep from * around: 24 sts
Rounds 2-3 knit
Round 4 *k2, ssk, k2tog, k2, rep from *around: 18 sts
Rounds 5-6 knit

Leaving sts on the needle(s), lightly stuff neck, head, and face.

Round 7 *k1, ssk, k2tog, k1, rep from * around: 12 sts
Rounds 8-9 knit
Round 10 [ssk, k2tog] 3 times: 6 sts

Add stuffing as necessary. Break yarn, thread tail through remaining sts, pull up and weave through.

EARS (worked flat, make 2)

CO 5.

Row 1 (and all odd-numbered rows) purl
Row 2 k1, kfb, k1, kfb, k1: 7 sts
Row 4 k2, kfb, k1, kfb, k2: 9 sts
Row 6 knit
Row 8 k2, ssk, k1, k2tog, k2: 7 sts
Row 10 k1, ssk, k1, k2tog, k1: 5 sts
Rows 12 ssk, k1, BO 1 st, k2tog, BO

Repeat for second ear.

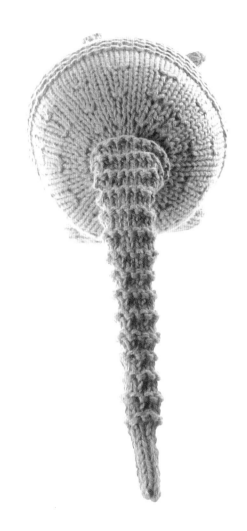

FEET (worked in the round, make 4)

CO 12. Join in a round.

Rounds 1-12 knit
Round 13 k2tog around: 6 sts

Break yarn, thread tail through remaining sts, pull up and weave through. Stuff front of foot. Repeat for other three feet.

TAIL (worked in the round)

Banding pattern:
Rounds 1-3 knit
Round 4 purl

CO 18. Join in a round.

Work 3 repeats of banding pattern.

Then, on round 2 of next repeat, decrease as follows:

*k2tog, k4, rep from * around: 15 sts

Continue working in banding pattern for 4 more repeats.

Then, on round 2 of the next repeat, decrease as follows:

*k2tog, k3, rep from * around: 12 sts

Continue working in banding pattern for 4 more repeats.

Then, on round 2 of the next repeat, decrease as follows:

*k2tog, k2, rep from * around: 9 sts

Then, on round 2 of the next repeat, decrease as follows:

*k2tog, k1, rep from * around: 6 sts

Work 9 rounds more. Then k2tog around: 3 sts

Break yarn, thread tail through remaining sts, pull up and weave through. (Tail is left unstuffed.)

ASSEMBLY AND FINISHING

Sew ears to crown as shown. Sew feet to belly as shown. Sew tail to bottom as shown. With black, make 2 French knot eyes.

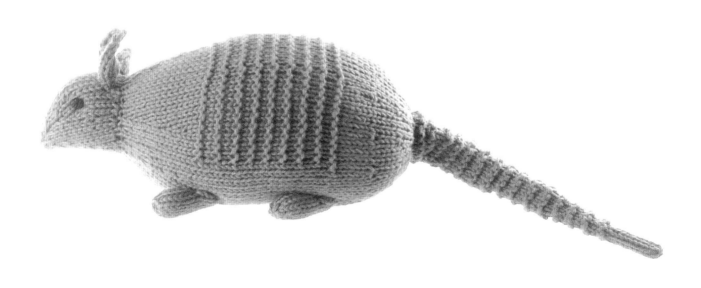

Coyote

Yarn
Brown Sheep Lamb's Pride Worsted colors M115 (Oatmeal), M02 (Brown Heather), and M05 (Onyx)

Yardage
Beige, 90 yds
Brown, 1 yd
Black, 1 yd

Measurements
Coyote is 8-1/2" tall.

Notes
1. Please read the Read Me First chapter, pp. 6-16 before you begin.

Instructions
Work basic bottom, p. 11, through round 10: 48 sts.

Body (continue working in the round)

Rounds 1-20 knit
Round 21 *k2, ssk, k8, k2tog, k2, rep from * around: 42 sts
Rounds 22-30 knit
Round 31 *k2, ssk, k6, k2tog, k2, rep from * around: 36 sts
Rounds 32-40 knit
Round 41 *k2, ssk, k4, k2tog, k2, rep from * around: 30 sts
Rounds 42-44 knit
Round 45 *k2, ssk, k2, k2tog, k2, rep from * around: 24 sts
Rounds 46-48 knit

Leaving sts on the needle(s), lightly stuff body.

Back neck (worked flat over 14 sts at center back)

Row 1 k7, turn
Row 2 sl1, p13
Row 3 sl1, k13

Repeat rounds 2 and 3 seven (7) times more.

SHAPE CROWN (short rows)

Row 1 sl1, p7, p2tog, p1, turn
Row 2 sl1, k3, ssk, k1, turn
Row 3 sl1, p4, p2tog, p1, turn
Row 4 sl1, k5, ssk, k1, turn
Row 5 sl1, p6, p2tog, p1, turn
Row 6 k7, ssk

Eight (8) sts remain in crown.

From the RS, pick up and knit 7 sts along left side of back neck; k1, [k2tog] 4 times, k1 across center front; pick up and knit 7 sts along right side of back neck, k4 from crown. Round (28 sts) now begins at center crown.

SHAPE FACE (worked in the round)

Round 1 knit
Round 2 k6, wrap the next st and turn, p12, wrap the next st and turn, k11, wrap the next st and turn, p10, wrap the next st and turn, k5 (to center).
Round 3 k5, knit the next 2 sts with their wraps, k14, knit the next 2 sts with their wraps, k5.

Leaving sts on the needle(s), lightly stuff neck, head, and face.

Round 4 k8, k2tog, k8, ssk, k8: 26 sts
Round 5 k10, [k2tog] 3 times, k10: 23 sts
Round 6 knit
Round 7 k5, [k2tog] twice, k5, [ssk] twice, k5: 19 sts
Round 8 knit
Round 9 k3, [k2tog] twice, k5, [ssk] twice, k3: 15 sts
Rounds 10-12 knit
Round 13 k1, [k2tog] twice, k5, [ssk] twice, k1: 11 sts
Rounds 14-15 knit

Leaving sts on the needle(s), lightly stuff nose.

Round 16 [k2tog] twice, k3, [ssk] twice: 7 sts

Add stuffing as necessary. Break yarn, thread tail through remaining sts, pull up and weave through.

EARS (worked flat, make 2)

CO 7.

Row 1 (and all odd-numbered rows) purl
Row 2 knit
Row 4 k2, cdd, k2: 5 sts
Row 6 k1, cdd, k1: 3 sts
Row 8 cdd: 1 st

BO. Repeat for second ear.

TAIL (worked in the round)

CO 6. Join in a round.

Rounds 1-6 knit
Round 7 kfb, k5: 7 sts
Rounds 8-10 knit
Round 11 k2, kfb, k3: 8 sts
Rounds 12-14 knit
Round 15 k6, kfb, k1: 9 sts
Rounds 16-33 knit

Leaving sts on the needle(s), lightly stuff tail.

Round 34 k2tog, k7: 8 sts
Round 35 k2, k2tog, k4: 7 sts
Round 36 k4, k2tog, k1: 6 sts

Add stuffing to tip of tail. Break yarn, thread tail through sts, pull up and weave through.

LEGS AND FEET (worked in the round, make 2)

CO 9. Join in a round.

Rounds 1-36 knit
Round 37 k2, [kfb] 5 times, k2: 14 sts
Rounds 38-41 knit
Round 42 k2, [k2tog] 5 times, k2: 9 sts
Round 43 *k2tog, k1, rep from * around: 6 sts

Break yarn, thread tail through remaining sts, pull up and weave through. Stuff foot and leg. Repeat for second leg and foot.

ASSEMBLY AND FINISHING

Sew ears to crown as shown. With brown, make a satin stitch nose. With black, make satin stitch eyes. Sew legs and tail to body as shown.

Instructions

Work basic bottom, p. 11, through round 10: 48 sts.

Body (continue working in the round)

Rounds 1-20 knit
Round 21 *k2, ssk, k8, k2tog, k2, rep from * around: 42 sts
Rounds 22-23 knit
Round 24 *k2, ssk, k6, k2tog, k2, rep from * around: 36 sts
Rounds 25-26 knit
Round 27 *k2, ssk, k4, k2tog, k2, rep from * around: 30 sts
Rounds 28-29 knit

Leaving sts on the needle(s), lightly stuff body.

Round 30 knit

Shape Crown (short rows)

Row 1 k8, wrap the next st and turn
Row 2 p16, wrap the next st and turn
Row 3 k15, wrap the next st and turn
Row 4 p14, wrap the next st and turn
Row 5 k13, wrap the next st and turn
Row 6 p12, wrap the next st and turn
Row 7 k11, wrap the next st and turn
Row 8 p10, wrap the next st and turn
Row 9 k9, wrap the next st and turn
Row 10 p8, wrap the next st and turn
Row 11 k7, wrap the next st and turn
Row 12 p6, wrap the next st and turn
Row 13 k3 (to center of crown)

Finish by knitting one round, as follows: k3, knit the next 6 sts with their wraps, k12, knit the next 6 sts with their wraps, k3.

Yarn

Brown Sheep Lamb's Pride Worsted colors M02 (Brown Heather), M34 (Victorian Pink), and M05 (Onyx)

Yardage

Brown, 85 yds
Pink, 2 yds
Black, 2 yds

Measurements

Javelina is 7" long.

Notes

1. Please read the Read Me First chapter, pp. 6-16 before you begin.

Face (continue working in the round)

Rounds 1-2 knit
Round 3 k1, ssk, k24, k2tog, k1: 28 sts
Round 4 knit
Round 5 k1, ssk, k22, k2tog, k1: 26 sts
Round 6 knit
Round 7 k1, ssk, k20, k2tog, k1: 24 sts
Round 8 knit

Leaving sts on the needle(s), lightly stuff neck, head, and face.

Round 9 *k1, ssk, k2, k2tog, k1, rep from * around: 18 sts

Rounds 10-11 knit
Round 12 *k1, ssk, k2tog, k1, rep from * around: 12 sts
Rounds 13-14 knit

Add stuffing as necessary. BO.

Snout (worked in the round)

With pink, CO 6. Join in a round.

Round 1 kfb around: 12 sts

BO loosely. Sew to opening at front of face.

Ears (worked flat, make 2)

CO 3.

Row 1 purl
Row 2 knit
Row 3 purl
Row 4 cdd: 1 st

BO. Repeat for second ear.

Legs and feet (worked in the round, make 4)

CO 9. Join in a round.

Rounds 1-20 knit
Round 21 k2, [kfb] twice, k1, [kfb] twice, k2: 13 sts
Rounds 22-25 knit
Round 26 k2, [k2tog] twice, k1, [k2tog] twice, k2: 9 sts
Round 27 *k2tog, k1, rep from * around: 6 sts

Break yarn, thread tail through remaining sts, pull up and weave through. Add stuffing to the foot, leaving leg unstuffed. With black sew a loop from the back of the foot at center, over the toe, and back to center back. Pull up tight and weave through. Repeat for each of three other legs and feet.

Assembly and finishing

Sew ears to crown as shown. Sew legs to body as shown. With black, make 2 satin stitch eyes.

Lizard

YARN

Brown Sheep Cotton Fleece colors CW555 (Robin Egg Blue), CW844 (Celery Leaves), CW345 (Gold Dust), and CW005 (Cavern)

YARDAGE

Aqua, 50 yds
Neon green, 3 yds
Gold, 20 yds
Black, 2 yds

MEASUREMENTS

Collared lizard is 15-1/2" long.

NOTES

1. Please read the Read Me First chapter, pp. 6-16 before you begin.

2. Use a smaller needle size with this yarn. Model was knit with US size 4 (3.5 mm) needles.

INSTRUCTIONS

TAIL AND BODY

Beginning at tail end, with aqua, CO 3. Work in I-cord, as follows:

Rounds 1-10 knit
Round 11 kfb, k2: 4 sts
Rounds 12-21 knit
Round 22 k2, kfb, k1: 5 sts
Rounds 23-32 knit
Round 33 k4, kfb: 6 sts
Join in a round and continue in rounds as follows:
Rounds 34-43 knit

128 Timeless Toys

Round 44 *kfb, k1, rep from * around: 9 sts

Begin lightly stuffing tail as you knit, about every 10 rounds.

Rounds 45-54 knit
Round 55 *kfb, k2, rep from * around: 12 sts
Rounds 56-65 knit
Round 66 *kfb, k3, rep from * around: 15 sts
Rounds 67-71 knit
Round 72 *kfb, k4, rep from * around: 18 sts
Rounds 73-77 knit
Round 78 *kfb, k5, rep from * around: 21 sts
Rounds 79-83 knit
Round 84 *kfb, k6, rep from * around: 24 sts
Rounds 85-89 knit
Round 90 *kfb, k7, rep from * around: 27 sts
Rounds 91-105 knit

Leaving sts on the needle(s), lightly stuff body.

Round 106 *k2, ssk, k1, k2tog, k2, rep from * around: 21 sts

HEAD (continue working in the round)

With black:

Round 1 knit

With gold:

Round 2 knit

With black:

Round 3 knit

With gold:

Round 4 *k3, kfb, k3, rep from * around: 24 sts
Round 5 knit
Round 6 k4, kfb, k1, kfb, k9, kfb, k1, kfb, k5: 28 sts
Round 7 k5, kfb, k1, kfb, k11, kfb, k1, kfb, k6: 32 sts
Round 8 knit

SHAPE CROWN (short rows)

Row 1 k5, wrap the next st and turn
Row 2 p10, wrap the next st and turn
Row 3 k9, wrap the next st and turn
Row 4 p8, wrap the next st and turn
Row 5 k4 (to center of crown)

Timeless Toys   129

FACE (worked in the round)

Round 1 k4, knit the next 2 sts with their wraps, k20, knit the next 2 sts with their wraps, k4
Round 2 k2tog, k28, ssk: 30 sts

Leaving sts on the needle(s), lightly stuff neck and head.

Round 3 k6, ssk, k2tog, k10, ssk, k2tog, k6: 26 sts
Round 4 knit
Round 5 k5, ssk, k2tog, k8, ssk, k2tog, k5: 22 sts
Round 6 knit
Round 7 k4, ssk, k2tog, k6, ssk, k2tog, k4: 18 sts
Round 8 knit
Round 9 k3, ssk, k2tog, k4, ssk, k2tog, k3: 14 sts
Round 10 knit
Round 11 k2, ssk, k2tog, k2, ssk, k2tog, k2: 10 sts
Round 12 knit

Leaving sts on the needle(s), lightly stuff face.

Round 13 k1, ssk, k2tog, ssk, k2tog, k1: 6 sts

Add stuffing as necessary. Break yarn, thread tail through remaining sts, pull up and weave through.

BACK LEGS (worked in the round, make 2)

CO 6. Join in a round.

Note: Gently stuff as you knit, about every 8 rounds.

Rounds 1-24 knit
Round 25 *kfb, k1, rep from * around: 9 sts
Rounds 26-45 knit

BO loosely. Stuff upper leg. Use small sts to secure bends in the leg and foot as shown. Tie two strands of neon green yarn through foot and secure them with square knots. Trim to about 3/8" for toes. Repeat for second back leg.

FRONT LEGS (worked in the round, make 2)

CO 6. Join in a round.

Note: Gently stuff as you knit, about every 8 rounds.

Rounds 1-30 knit

BO loosely. Use small sts to secure bends in leg and foot as shown. Tie two strands of neon green yarn through foot and secure them with square knots. Trim to about 3/8" for toes. Repeat for second front leg.

ASSEMBLY AND FINISHING

Sew legs to body as shown. With black, make 2 straight stitch eyes. With neon green yarn, use duplicate stitches to work random stripes on back as shown.

Prairie Dog

Yarn
Brown Sheep Lamb's Pride Worsted colors M08 (Wild Oak) and M05 (Onyx)

Yardage
Tan, 50 yds
Black, 1/2 yd

Measurements
Prairie dog is 7-1/2" tall.

Notes
1. Please read the Read Me First chapter, pp. 6-16 before you begin.

Instructions
Work basic bottom, p. 11, through round 6: 36 sts.

Body (continue working in the round)

Rounds 1-40 knit
Round 41 *k2, ssk, k4, k2tog, k2, rep from * around: 30 sts
Rounds 42-44 knit
Round 45 *k2, ssk, k2, k2tog, k2, rep from * around: 24 sts
Round 46 knit

Leaving sts on the needle(s), lightly stuff body.

Round 47 k6, [k2tog] 6 times, k6: 18 sts

Back neck (worked flat over 12 sts at center back)

Row 1 k6, turn
Row 2 sl1, p11
Row 3 sl1, k11

Repeat rounds 2 and 3 seven times more.

Shape crown (short rows)

Row 1 sl1, p6, p2tog, p1, turn
Row 2 sl1, k3, ssk, k1, turn
Row 3 sl1, p4, p2tog, p1, turn
Row 4 sl1, k5, ssk, k1

Eight (8) sts remain in crown.

From the RS, pick up and knit 9 sts along left side of back neck; knit across 6 sts at center front; pick up and knit 9 sts along right side of back neck, k4 from crown. Round (32 sts) now begins at center crown.

SHAPE FACE (worked in the round)

Round 1 k1, ssk, k7, k2tog, k8, ssk, k7, k2tog, k1: 28 sts
Round 2 knit
Round 3 k8, k2tog, k8, ssk, k8: 26 sts
Round 4 knit
Round 5 k7, k2tog, k8, ssk, k7: 24 sts
Round 6 knit

Leaving sts on the needle(s), lightly stuff neck, head, and face.

Round 7 *k1, ssk, k2, k2tog, k1, rep from * around: 18 sts
Rounds 8-9 knit
Round 10 *k1, ssk, k2tog, k1, rep from * around: 12 sts
Rounds 11-12 knit
Round 13 k2tog around: 6 sts

Add stuffing as necessary. Break yarn, thread tail through remaining sts, pull up and weave through.

EARS (worked flat, make 2)

CO 3.

Row 1 purl
Row 2 cdd: 1 st

BO. Repeat for second ear.

TAIL (worked in the round)

CO 6. Join in a round.

Rounds 1-24 knit

Break yarn, thread tail through sts, pull up and weave through.

FEET (worked in the round, make 2)

CO 9. Join in a round

Rounds 1-10 knit
Round 11 *k2tog, k1, rep from * around: 6 sts

Break yarn, thread tail through remaining sts, pull up and weave through. Stuff front of foot for paw. Repeat for second foot.

ARMS (worked in the round, make 2)

CO 6. Join in a round.

Rounds 1-12 knit

Break yarn, thread tail through sts, pull up and weave through. Stuff front of arm for paw.

Repeat for second arm.

ASSEMBLY AND FINISHING

Sew ears to crown as shown. With tan, make a satin stitch nose. With black, make satin stitch eyes. Sew arms, feet, and tail to body as shown.

Wetlands

Growing up in the country gave me lots of opportunities for poking about in streams and ponds. Every child will love to tuck in the turtle's parts and then pull them back out of its shell.

Beaver

Yarn

Brown Sheep Lamb's Pride Worsted colors M175 (Bronze Patina), M02 (Brown Heather), M11 (White Frost), and M05 (Onyx)

Yardage

Dark brown, 70 yds
Light brown, 24 yds
White and black, 1 yd each

Measurements

Beaver is 5-3/4".

Notes

1. Please read the Read Me First chapter, pp. 6-16 before you begin.

Instructions

Work basic bottom, p. 11, through round 15: 60 sts.

Body (continue working in the round)

Rounds 1-5 knit
Round 6 *k2, ssk, k12, k2tog, k2, rep from * around: 54 sts
Rounds 7-9 knit
Round 10 *k2, ssk, k10, k2tog, k2, rep from * around: 48 sts
Rounds 11-13 knit
Round 14 *k2, ssk, k8, k2tog, k2, rep from * around: 42 sts
Rounds 15-17 knit
Round 18 *k2, ssk, k6, k2tog, k2, rep from * around: 36 sts
Round 19 knit
Round 20 *k2, ssk, k4, k2tog, k2, rep from * around: 30 sts
Round 21 knit
Round 22 *k2, ssk, k2, k2tog, k2, rep from * around: 24 sts
Round 23 knit

Leaving sts on the needle(s), lightly stuff body.

Neck and head (continue working in the round)

Round 1 [kfb] 8 times, [k2tog] 4 times, [kfb] 8 times: 36 sts
Round 2 knit
Round 3 k14, ssk, k4, k2tog, k14: 34 sts
Round 4 knit
Round 5 k11, [ssk] twice, k4, [k2tog] twice, k11: 30 sts
Round 6 knit

Shape crown (short rows)

Row 1 k4, wrap the next st and turn
Row 2 p8, wrap the next st and turn
Row 3 k7, wrap the next st and turn
Row 4 p6, wrap the next st and turn
Row 5 k5, wrap the next st and turn
Row 6 p4, wrap the next st and turn
Row 7 k2 (to beginning of round)

Shape face (continue working in the round)

Round 1 k7, working wraps with corresponding sts, [ssk] 4 times, [k2tog] 4 times, k7, working wraps with corresponding sts: 22 sts
Round 2 ssk, k18, k2tog: 20 sts
Round 3 knit
Round 4 [ssk] twice, k1, [ssk] twice, k2, [k2tog] twice, k1, [k2tog] twice: 12 sts
Round 5 knit

Leaving sts on the needle(s), lightly stuff neck, head, and face.

Round 6 ssk, k8, k2tog: 10 sts
Round 7 knit
Round 8 ssk, k6, k2tog: 8 sts

Leaving sts on the needle(s), stuff nose. With 4 sts on top and 4 sts on bottom, use the Kitchener stitch to graft the nose.

Ears (worked flat, make 2)

CO 5.

Row 1 purl
Row 2 ssk, k1, k2tog: 3 sts
Row 3 purl
Row 4 ssk, k1: 2 sts

BO. Rep for second ear.

Tail (worked flat)

With light brown, CO 7.

Row 1 knit
Row 2 kfb, k4, kfb, k1: 9 sts
Rows 3-7 knit
Row 8 kfb, k6, kfb, k1: 11 sts
Rows 9-17 knit
Row 18 kfb, k8, kfb, k1: 13 sts
Rows 19-37 knit
Row 38 kfb, k10, kfb, k1: 15 sts
Rows 39-47 knit
Row 48 k1, ssk, k9, k2tog, k1: 13 sts
Row 49 knit
Row 50 k1, ssk, k7, k2tog, k1: 11 sts
Row 51 knit
Row 52 k1, ssk, k5, k2tog, k1: 9 sts
Row 53 knit
Row 54 k1, ssk, k3, k2tog, k1: 7 sts

BO.

Pick up and knit sts around all but the CO edge (one st behind each garter ridge on long sides; one st for each bound-off st). From the RS, BO as follows: *k2tog tbl, replace st from right hand needle to left hand needle, rep from * around.

BACK FEET (worked flat, make 2)

CO 13.

Row 1 k6, p1, k6
Row 2 k5, cdd, k5: 11 sts
Row 3 k5, p1, k5
Row 4 knit
Row 5 rep row 3
Row 6 k4, cdd, k4: 9 sts
Row 7 k4, p1, k4
Row 8 knit
Row 9 rep row 7
Row 10 k3, cdd, k3: 7 sts
Row 11 k3, p1, k3
Row 12 knit
Row 13 rep row 11
Row 14 k2, cdd, k2: 5 sts
Row 15 k2, p1, k2
Row 16 k1, cdd, k1: 3 sts
Row 17 k1, p1, k1
Row 18 cdd: 1 st

BO. Repeat for second foot.

ARMS AND FRONT PAWS (worked in the round, make 2)

CO 6. Join in a round.

Rounds 1-10 knit
Round 11 k1, [kfb] 4 times, k1: 10 sts
Rounds 12-15 knit
Round 16 k1, [k2tog] 4 times, k1: 6 sts

Break yarn, thread tail through remaining sts, pull up and weave through. Stuff just the paw. Repeat for second arm and paw.

ASSEMBLY AND FINISHING

Sew ears to crown as shown. With black, make a satin stitch nose as shown. With white, using satin stitch, make two teeth as shown. With black, using a lazy-daisy stitch, make two eyes as shown. Sew tail to bottom of back as shown. Sew feet to bottom of body. Sew arms to body as shown. Tack paws together if desired.

Frog

Yarn
Brown Sheep Lamb's Pride Worsted colors M120 (Limeade) and M05 (Onyx)

Yardage
Green, 60 yds
Black, 1 yd

Measurements
Frog is 6" long, from nose to tail.

Notes
1. Please read the Read Me First chapter, pp. 6-16 before you begin.

Instructions
Work bird bottom, p. 11: 42 sts.

Body (worked in the round)

Rounds 1-6 knit
Round 7 k9, k2tog, k4, ssk, k8, k2tog, k4, ssk, k9: 38 sts
Rounds 8-10 knit
Round 11 k8, k2tog, k4, ssk, k6, k2tog, k4, ssk, k8: 34 sts
Rounds 12-14 knit
Round 15 k7, k2tog, k4, ssk, k4, k2tog, k4, ssk, k7: 30 sts
Rounds 16-18 knit
Round 19 *k2, ssk, k2, k2tog, k2, rep from * around: 24 sts
Round 20 k6, [k2tog] 6 times, k6: 18 sts

Leaving sts on the needle(s), lightly stuff body and tail.

Head (continue in the round)

Round 1 k5, [kfb] twice, k4, [kfb] twice, k5: 22 sts
Round 2 knit
Round 3 k6, [kfb] twice, k6, [kfb] twice, k6: 26 sts
Round 4 knit
Round 5 k7, [kfb] twice, k8, [kfb] twice, k7: 30 sts
Round 6 knit

Shape crown (short rows)

Row 1 k5, wrap the next st and turn
Row 2 p10, wrap the next st and turn
Row 3 k9, wrap the next st and turn
Row 4 p8, wrap the next st and turn
Row 5 k7, wrap the next st and turn
Row 6 p6, purling in wraps with corresponding sts, wrap the next st and turn
Row 7 k3 (to center crown)

Finish by knitting one round as follows: k3, knit the next 3 sts with their wraps, k18, knit the next 3 sts with their wraps, k3.

Shape face (continue in the round)

Round 1 [k2tog] twice, k3, ssk, k2tog, k8, ssk, k2tog, k3, [ssk] twice: 22 sts
Round 2 knit
Round 3 k4, ssk, k2tog, k6, ssk, k2tog, k4: 18 sts
Round 4 knit
Round 5 k3, ssk, k2tog, k4, ssk, k2tog, k3: 14 sts
Round 6 knit

Leaving sts on the needle(s), lightly stuff head and face.

Round 7 k1, ssk, k2tog, k4, ssk, k2tog, k1: 10 sts

Leaving sts on the needle(s), add stuffing to face as necessary. With 5 sts on the top and 5 sts on the bottom, use the Kitchener stitch to graft the mouth.

Back legs and feet (worked flat, finished in I-cord)

CO 15.

Row 1 k6, cdd, k6: 13 sts
Row 2 k6, p1, k6
Row 3 k5, cdd, k5: 11 sts
Row 4 k5, p1, k5
Row 5 k4, cdd, k4: 9 sts
Row 6 k4, p1, k4
Row 7 k3, cdd, k3: 7 sts
Row 8 k3, p1, k3
Row 9 k2, cdd, k2: 5 sts
Row 10 k2, p1, k2
Row 11 k1, cdd, k1: 3 sts

Without turning work, continue leg in 3-st I-cord for 6 rows.

On the next row, [kfb] twice, k1: 5 sts.

Continue in 5-st I-cord for 9 rows.

On the next row, k1, kfb, k1, kfb, k1: 7 sts.

Continue in 7-st I-cord for 20 rows.

BO. Repeat for second back leg and foot.

FRONT LEGS AND FEET (worked flat, finished in I-cord)

CO 11.

Row 1 k4, cdd, k4: 9 sts
Row 2 k4, p1, k4
Row 3 k3, cdd, k3: 7 sts
Row 4 k3, p1, k3
Row 5 k2, cdd, k2: 5 sts
Row 6 k2, p1, k2
Row 7 k1, cdd, k1: 3 sts

Without turning work, continue leg in 3-st I-cord for 1 row.

On the next row, k1, kfb, k1: 4 sts.

Continue in 4-st I-cord for 12 rows.

BO.

Repeat for second front leg and foot.

EYES (worked flat, make 2)

CO 1.

Row 1 knit in the front, the back, and the front of the st: 3 sts
Row 2 pfb, p1, pfb: 5 sts
Row 3 knit
Row 4 p2tog, p1, p2tog: 3 sts

BO, working a k2tog with the first 2 sts. Place a small amount of stuffing on the WS. Tie the tails together in back. Thread a tapestry needle with one of the tails, and thread the tail through an edge opposite the cast on and bind off points. Repeat with second tail. Tie these ends gently over the first knot, rounding out the eye. Repeat for second eye.

ASSEMBLY AND FINISHING

Sew back legs and feet in place, as shown. Sew front legs and feet in place as shown. Tack front legs (at foot) to front of frog if desired. Use one of the tails to sew the eye in place on the side of the crown, as shown. With black, make a French knot in the center of the eye. Repeat for second eye.

Garter Snake

Yarn

Brown Sheep Cotton Fleece colors CW005 (Cavern), CW725 (Buttercream), and CW440 (Spanish Olive)

Yardage

Black, 50 yds
Yellow, 15 yds
Green, 15 yds

Measurements

Snake is ~16" long.

Notes

1. Please read the Read Me First chapter, pp. 6-16 before you begin.

2. Use a smaller needle size with this yarn. Model was knit with US size 4 (3.5 mm) needles.

Instructions

Head (worked in the round)

With black, CO 6. Join in a round. (Round begins and ends at the center of the top of the head.)

Round 1 knit
Round 2 kfb around: 12 sts
Rounds 3-7 knit
Round 8 k3, [kfb] twice, k2, [kfb] twice, k3: 16 sts
Rounds 9-10 knit
Round 11 k3, [k2tog] twice, k2, [k2tog] twice, k3: 12 sts
Round 12 knit

Leaving sts on the needle(s), stuff head.

Body (continued in the round, stuffing as you go)

Continue knitting rounds, stuffing every 10 rounds or so, until snake measures 6" from nose.

Work a decrease round as follows:

k2tog, k8, ssk: 10 sts

Continue as before, until snake measures 12" from nose. Work a decrease round as follows:

k2tog, k6, ssk: 8 sts

Continue as before, until snake measures 14-1/2" from nose. Work a decrease round as follows:

k2tog, k4, ssk: 6 sts

Continue as before, until snake measures 16". Work a decrease round as follows:

k2tog around onto one needle: 3 sts

Continue in 3-st I-cord for 3 rounds.

BO.

Finishing

With yellow, make two lazy-daisy stitch eyes as shown. With green, make straight stitches around eyes as shown. With black, add a French knot to the center of each eye. Make running stitch stripes down center of back using yellow and green as shown. Cut a strand of yellow about 8" long. Double thread a tapestry needle. Go into the snake's body stuffing about 3" behind nose. Come out at center of nose and clip ends to about 3/8" for forked tongue.

To make the snake "snaky," use a strand of black knotted onto a bar between stitches at the side of the snake and weave in and out of the bars between sts at the side. Pull up and tie off. Repeat on the opposite side of the snake for the next curve, and so on, until your snake curves as you would like. Note: This is in lieu of short rows, and considerably easier, though not quite as durable.

Snail

Yarn
Noro Kureyon Worsted
color 262

Yardage
Shell, 10 yds
Head, 5 yds
Foot, 2 yds
Eyes, 1/2 yd black or a very dark color

If working from one ball of Kureyon, as I did, you will need about 18 yards total. The shell is worked self-striped. Choose light and dark bits for the other pieces.

Measurements
Snail is 2" tall and 3-1/2" long.

Notes
1. Please read the Read Me First chapter, pp. 6-16 before you begin.

Instructions

Shell (worked in the round)
CO 9. Join in a round. Knit 10 rounds. Use the CO tail to close the tube, and lightly stuff. Knit 40 rounds more, lightly stuffing every 10 rounds or so.

Shape opening
Round 1 *k1, kfb, rep from * around: 12 sts
Rounds 2-5 knit

BO loosely. Do not stuff this portion of the shell.

Neck and head (worked in the round)
CO 9. Join in a round.

Rounds 1-5 knit
Round 6 k1, kfb, k5, kfb, k1: 11 sts
Round 7 knit
Round 8 k1, k2tog, k5, k2tog, k1: 9 sts
Rounds 9-10 knit
Round 11 *k1, k2tog, rep from * around: 6 sts

Break yarn, thread tail through remaining sts, pull up and weave through. Lightly stuff neck and head.

Foot (worked in the round, make 2)
CO 6. Join in a round.

Round 1 kfb around: 12 sts
Round 2 knit
BO.

Horns (make 2)

CO 2.

Work in 2-st I-cord for 5 rows.

BO. Repeat for second horn.

Assembly and finishing

Beginning with the CO end of the shell, start coiling the shell, using the CO tail to stitch the coil together at its center (inside the coil). Insert neck into the unstuffed, flared opening of the shell, and tack neck in place to the BO row of the shell. Sew horns to top of head. Sew foot to bottom of shell, where shell meets neck. With black, make a straight-stitch eye on each side of the head, in front of the horns.

Turtle

Yarn
Brown Sheep Lamb's Pride Worsted colors M08 (Wild Oak), M171 (Fresh Moss), M13 (Sun Yellow), M22 (Autumn Harvest), and M05 (Onyx)

Yardage
Brown, 35 yds
Green, 65 yds
Yellow, 15 yds
Orange, 2 yds
Black, 1 yd

Measurements
Turtle is 3" tall and 8" long.

Notes
1. Please read the Read Me First chapter, pp. 6-16 before you begin.

Instructions

Top shell
With brown, Work basic bottom, p. 11, through round 15: 60 sts.

Continue in the round:

Rounds 16-20 knit
Rounds 21-23 *p4, k1, rep from * around

BO loosely in knit.

Lining
With green, work basic bottom through round 15: 60 sts.

Continue in the round:

Rounds 16-19 knit

BO.

Stuff top shell, leaving a depression in the center of the stuffing. With RSs out (WSs facing), sew lining edge to inside of top shell, just above purl rounds. With orange use a running stitch to create an accent row around the top shell as shown.

Bottom shell (worked flat)
With yellow, CO 17.

Pattern stitch:
Rows 1-7 knit
Row 8 purl

Note: On the first pattern repeat only, start with row 2.

Work in pattern stitch, increasing on the first three RS rows (rows 3, 5, and 7), as follows: k1, kfb, k to last 3 sts, kfb, k2: 23 sts.

Continue in pattern on 23 sts until four pattern repeats have been worked. Continuing in established pattern, decrease on 3, 5, and 7, as follows: k1, ssk, k to last 3 sts, k2tog, k1: 17 sts.

BO on row 7.

Tail (worked as I-cord)

With green, CO 6. Work in I-cord for 10 rows.

On the next row:

k1, ssk, k2tog, k1: 4 sts.

Continue in I-cord for three more rows.

On the next row:

ssk, k2tog: 2 sts.

Work one more row of I-cord. BO.

Neck and head (worked in the round)

With green, CO 12. Join in a round.

Rounds 1-12 knit
Round 13 k2, [kfb] twice, k4, [kfb] twice, k2: 16 sts
Rounds 14-17 knit
Round 18 k2, [k2tog] twice, k4, [ssk] twice, k2: 12 sts
Round 19 knit
Round 20 k2tog around: 6 sts

Break yarn, thread tail through remaining sts, pull up and weave through. Lightly stuff head, leaving neck unstuffed.

ASSEMBLY AND FINISHING

Sew neck, tail, and legs to lining of top shell ~1/2" in from edge of lining. Sew bottom shell to the seam that joins top shell with lining, tacking only several stitches between appendages. This will allow head, tail, and legs and feet to be tucked into the shell, like a real turtle.

FEATURES

With yellow, work two loose lazy-daisy stitch eyes. With black, make a French knot inside each eye. With orange, use straight stitches to emphasize eyes, as shown.

LEGS AND FEET (worked in the round, make 4)

With green, CO 9.

Rounds 1-12 knit
Round 13 k3, [kfb] 3 times, k3: 12 sts
Rounds 14-17 knit
Round 18 k3, [k2tog] 3 times, k3: 9 sts
Round 20 *k1, k2tog, rep from * around: 6 sts

Break yarn, thread tail through remaining sts, pull up and weave through. Stuff foot, leaving leg unstuffed. Repeat for other legs and feet.

Woodlands
*Woodlands vary a bit across this huge country of ours and around the world. These guys are the residents in **my** backyard.*

Mouse

YARN
Brown Sheep Nature Spun Worsted colors 701 (Stone) and 601 (Pepper)

YARDAGE
Brown, 30 yds
Black, 1/2 yd

MEASUREMENTS
Mouse is 2-1/2" long, excluding tail.

NOTES
1. Please read the Read Me First chapter, pp. 6-16 before you begin.

INSTRUCTIONS
Work basic bottom, p. 11, through round 6: 36 sts.

BODY (continue working in the round)

Rounds 1-11 knit
Round 12 *k2tog, k8, ssk, rep from * around: 30 sts
Rounds 13-15 knit
Round 16 *k2tog, k6, ssk, rep from * around: 24 sts

Leaving sts on the needle(s), lightly stuff.

Rounds 17-19 knit
Round 20 *k2tog, k4, ssk, rep from * around: 18 sts
Rounds 21-23 knit
Round 24 *k2tog, k2, ssk, rep from * around: 12 sts

Leaving sts on the needle(s), lightly stuff.

Round 25 knit
Round 26 *k2tog, ssk, rep from * around: 6 sts

Leaving sts on the needle(s), lightly stuff body. Break yarn, thread tail through remaining sts, pull up and weave through.

Tail

CO 3. Work in 3-st I-cord until tail measures 5″. BO.

Ears (worked flat, make 2)

CO 5. Turn.

Row 1 p1, pfb, p1, pfb, p1: 7 sts
Row 2 knit
Row 3 purl
Row 4 knit
Row 5 p1, p2tog, p1, p2tog, p1: 5 sts
Row 6 knit
Row 7 p2tog, p1, p2tog: 3 sts
Row 8 cdd: 1 st

BO. Repeat for second ear.

Assembly and finishing

Sew tail to back. Sew ears to side of head as shown. With black, make duplicate stitch eyes and a satin stitch nose.

Owl and Owlets

Yarn
Brown Sheep Nature Spun Worsted colors 720 (Ash), 209 (Wood Moss), and 305 (Impasse Yellow)

Yardage
Tan: Owl, 50 yds; Owlets (each), 28 yds
Brown: Owl, 10 yds; Owlets (each), 5 yds
Yellow: Owl, 5 yds; Owlets (each), 3 yds

Measurements
Owl is 6" tall; owlets are 3" tall.

Notes
1. Please read the Read Me First chapter, pp. 6-16 before you begin.

Owl Instructions
With tan, work basic bottom, p. 11, through round 15: 60 sts.

Body (continue working in the round)

Rounds 1-24 knit
Round 25 *k2, ssk, k12, k2tog, k2, rep from * around: 54 sts
Rounds 26-28 knit
Round 29 *k2, ssk, k10, k2tog, k2, rep from * around: 48 sts
Rounds 30-32 knit
Round 33 *k2tog, k2, rep from * around: 36 sts
Rounds 34-35 knit
Round 36 *k2tog, k1, rep from * around: 24 sts
Round 37 knit

Leaving sts on the needle(s), stuff body.

Round 38 k2tog around: 12 sts
Round 39 knit
Round 40 k2tog around: 6 sts

Add stuffing as necessary. Break yarn, thread tail through remaining sts, pull up and weave through.

Eyes (worked in the round, make 2)

With yellow, CO 6. Join in a round.
Round 1 kfb around: 12 sts
Round 2 knit

BO loosely.

Repeat for second eye.

Horns (worked flat, make 2)

With tan, CO 5.

Rows 1-2 knit
Row 3 ssk, k1, k2tog: 3 sts
Row 4 knit
Row 5 cdd: 1 st

BO. Repeat for second horn.

Beak (worked flat)

With brown, CO 2.

Row 1 [kfb] twice: 4 sts
Rows 5-10 knit
Row 11 *kfb, k1, rep from *: 6 sts

BO.

Assembly and finishing

Sew eyes and beak to front of face. With brown, work satin stitch pupils. Sew horns to crown as shown.

Owlet Instructions

With tan, Work basic bottom, p. 11, through round 6: 36 sts.

Body (continue working in the round)

Rounds 1-17 knit
Round 18 *k2, ssk, k4, k2tog, k2, rep from * around: 30 sts
Rounds 19-21 knit
Round 22 *k2, ssk, k2, k2tog, k2, rep from * around: 24 sts
Rounds 23-24 knit

Leaving sts on the needle(s), lightly stuff body.

Round 25 k2tog around: 12 sts
Round 26 knit
Round 27 k2tog around: 6 sts

Add stuffing as necessary. Break yarn, thread tail through remaining sts, pull up and weave through.

Eyes (worked in the round, make 2)

With yellow, CO 6. Join in a round.
Round 1 *kfb, k1, rep from * around: 9 sts

BO loosely.

Repeat for second eye.

Horns (worked flat, make 2)

With tan, CO 3.

Row 1 purl
Row 2 knit
Row 3 p2tog, p1: 2 sts

BO. Repeat for second horn.

Beak (worked flat)

With brown, CO 1.
Row 1 kfb: 2 sts
Row 2 kfb, k1: 3 sts
Rows 3-7 knit
Row 8 kfb, k1, kfb: 5 sts

BO.

Assembly and finishing

Sew eyes and beak to front of face. With brown, make French knot pupils. Sew horns to crown as shown.

Rabbit

YARN
Brown Sheep Nature Spun Worsted colors N03 (Grey Heather), 701 (Stone), and 740 (Snow)

YARDAGE
Grey, 65 yds
Brown and white, 1 yd each

MEASUREMENTS
Rabbit is 7" long.

NOTES
1. Please read the Read Me First chapter, pp. 6-16 before you begin.

INSTRUCTIONS
Work basic bottom, p. 11, through round 15: 60 sts.

BODY (continue working in the round)

Rounds 1-8 knit
Round 9 *k2, k2tog, k12, ssk, k2, rep from * around: 54 sts
Rounds 10-14 knit
Round 15 *k2, k2tog, k10, ssk, k2, rep from * around: 48 sts
Rounds 16-20 knit
Round 21 *k2, k2tog, k8, ssk, k2, rep from * around: 42 sts
Rounds 22-24 knit
Round 25 *k2, k2tog, k6, ssk, k2, rep from * around: 36 sts
Rounds 26-28 knit
Round 29 *k2, k2tog, k4, ssk, k2, rep from * around: 30 sts
Rounds 30-32 knit
Round 33 *k2, k2tog, k2, ssk, k2, rep from * around: 24 sts
Round 34 knit

Leaving sts on the needle(s), lightly stuff body.

HEAD (continue working in the round)

Round 1 [kfb] 6 times, [k2tog] 6 times, [kfb] 6 times: 30 sts
Round 2 knit
Round 3 k8, wrap the next st and turn; p16, wrap the next st and turn; k14, wrap the next st and turn; p12, wrap the next st and turn; k6
Round 4 knit, knitting in wraps with their corresponding sts
Round 5 k2, ssk, k6, k2tog, k6, ssk, k6,

k2tog, k2: 26 sts
Round 6 knit
Round 7 k2, ssk, k18, k2tog, k2: 24 sts
Round 8 knit
Round 9 k2, ssk, k3, k2tog, k6, ssk, k3, k2tog, k2: 20 sts
Round 10 knit
Round 11 k2, ssk, k2tog, k8, ssk, k2tog, k2: 16 sts

Leaving sts on the needle(s), lightly stuff head.

Round 12 k6, ssk, k2tog, k6: 14 sts
Round 13 knit
Round 14 k2tog around: 7 sts

Add stuffing to nose as necessary. Break yarn, thread tail through remaining sts, pull up and weave through.

Ears (worked flat, make 2)

CO 9.

Row 1 (and all odd-numbered rows) purl
Row 2 knit
Row 4 k2, ssk, k1, k2tog, k2: 7 sts
Rows 6 and 8 knit
Row 10 k1, ssk, k1, k2tog, k1: 5 sts
Rows 12 and 14 knit
Row 16 ssk, k1, k2tog: 3 sts
Row 18 k1, k2tog: 2 sts

BO. Repeat for second ear.

Tail (worked flat)

With grey, CO 5.

Row 1 (and all odd-numbered rows) purl
Row 2 k1, kfb, k1, kfb, k1: 7 sts
Rows 4 and 6 knit

Switch to white for row 8.

Rows 8 and 10 knit
Row 12 k1, ssk, k1, k2tog, k1: 5 sts

BO. Sew a short seam on both sides of the tail so that the front is grey and the back is white. Lightly stuff tail.

Back feet (worked in the round, make 2)

CO 15. Join in a round.

Rounds 1-10 knit
Round 11 *k2tog, k1, k2tog, rep from * around: 9 sts
Round 12 *k2tog, k1, rep from * around: 6 sts

Break yarn, thread tail through remaining sts, pull up and weave through. Stuff the front part of the foot, leaving the back, open end unstuffed. Repeat for second back foot.

Front feet (worked in the round, make 2)

CO 9. Join in a round.

Rounds 1-10 knit
Round 11 *k2tog, k1, rep from * around: 6 sts.

Break yarn, thread tail through remaining sts, pull up and weave through. Stuff the front part of the foot, leaving the back, open end unstuffed. Repeat for second front foot.

Assembly and finishing

Sew tail, ears, and feet in place as shown. With light brown, make 2 French knot eyes and a satin stitch nose.

Skunk

Yarn

Brown Sheep Nature Spun Worsted colors 601 (Pepper) and 740 (Snow)

Yardage

Black, 90 yds
White, 15 yds

Measurements

Skunk is 7-1/2" long and 8" tall at the tail.

Notes

1. Please read the Read Me First chapter, pp. 6-16 before you begin.

Instructions

Work basic bottom, p. 11, through round 15: 60 sts.

Body (continue working in the round)

Rounds 1-8 knit
Round 9 *k2, k2tog, k12, ssk, k2, rep from * around: 54 sts
Rounds 10-14 knit
Round 15 *k2, k2tog, k10, ssk, k2, rep from * around: 48 sts
Rounds 16-20 knit
Round 21 *k2, k2tog, k8, ssk, k2, rep from * around: 42 sts
Rounds 22-24 knit
Round 25 *k2, k2tog, k6, ssk, k2, rep from * around: 36 sts
Rounds 26-28 knit
Round 29 *k2, k2tog, k4, ssk, k2, rep from * around: 30 sts
Rounds 30-32 knit

Leaving sts on the needle(s), lightly stuff body.

Round 33 k6, [k2tog] 9 times, k6: 21 sts

Head (continue working in the round)

Round 1 [kfb] 6 times, k9, [kfb] 6 times: 33 sts
Rounds 2-3 knit
Round 4 k10, wrap the next st and turn; p20, wrap the next st and turn; k10
Round 5 k10, knit the next st with its wrap, k11, knit the next st with its wrap, k10
Rounds 6-9 Rep rounds 4 and 5 twice more
Round 10 k2, ssk, k6, k2tog, k2, ssk, k1,

k2tog, k2, ssk, k6, k2tog, k2: 27 sts
Round 11 knit
Round 12 k2, ssk, k4, k2tog, k7, ssk, k4, k2tog, k2: 23 sts
Round 13 knit
Round 14 k2, ssk, k2, k2tog, k7, ssk, k2, k2tog, k2: 19 sts
Round 15 knit

Leaving sts on the needle(s), lightly stuff head and face.

Round 16 [k2tog] 4 times, k3, [k2tog] 4 times: 11 sts
Rounds 17-18 knit
Round 19 [k2tog] twice, k3, [k2tog] twice: 7 sts

Add stuffing to nose as necessary. Break yarn, thread tail through remaining sts, pull up and weave through.

Stripes: With white, make chain stitch stripes on body and head as shown.

TAIL (worked in the round)

CO 20. Join in a round.

Rounds 1-3 knit
Round 4 *kfb, k7, kfb, k1, rep from *: 24 sts
Round 5 knit
Round 6 *kfb, k9, kfb, k1, rep from *: 28 sts
Rounds 7-26 knit
Round 27 *k2tog, k10, ssk, rep from *: 24 sts
Rounds 28-30 knit

Round 31 *k2tog, k8, ssk, rep from *: 20 sts
Rounds 32-34 knit
Round 35 *k2tog, k6, ssk, rep from *: 16 sts
Rounds 36-38 knit
Round 39 *k2tog, k4, ssk, rep from *: 12 sts
Rounds 40-42 knit
Round 43 k2tog around: 6 sts

Break yarn, thread tail through remaining sts, pull up and weave through. Lightly stuff tail.

Stripes: With white, make chain stitch stripes on tail shown.

EARS (worked flat, make 2)

CO 3.

Row 1 purl
Row 2 knit
Row 3 purl
Row 4 k2tog, k1: 2 sts

BO. Repeat for second ear.

FEET (worked in the round, make 4)

CO 9. Join in a round.

Rounds 1-10 knit
Round 11 *k2tog, k1, rep from * around: 6 sts.

Break yarn, thread tail through remaining sts, pull up and weave through. Stuff the front part of the foot, leaving the back, open end unstuffed. Repeat for other three feet.

ASSEMBLY AND FINISHING

Sew tail, ears, and feet in place as shown. With black, make 2 French knot eyes and a satin stitch nose.

Timeless Toys 155

Squirrel

Yarn

Brown Sheep Nature Spun Worsted colors 124 (Butterscotch), 148 (Autumn Leaves), 701 (Stone), and 601 (Pepper)

Yardage

Dark brown, 100 yds
Green, 5 yds
Light brown, 3 yds
Black, 1/2 yd

Measurements

Squirrel stands 6-1/2" tall

Notes

1. Please read the Read Me First chapter, pp. 6-16 before you begin.

Instructions

Work basic bottom, p. 11, through round 15: 60 sts.

Body (continue working in the round)

Rounds 1-8 knit
Round 9 *k2, ssk, k12, k2tog, k2, rep from * around: 54 sts
Rounds 10-14 knit
Round 15 *k2, ssk, k10, k2tog, k2, rep from * around: 48 sts
Rounds 16-20 knit
Round 21 *k2, ssk, k8, k2tog, k2, rep from * around: 42 sts
Rounds 22-24 knit
Round 25 *k2, ssk, k6, k2tog, k2, rep from * around: 36 sts
Rounds 26-28 knit
Round 29 *k2, ssk, k4, k2tog, k2, rep from * around: 30 sts
Rounds 30-32 knit
Round 33 *k2, ssk, k2, k2tog, k2, rep from * around: 24 sts

Leaving sts on the needle(s), lightly stuff body.

Neck and head (continue working in the round)

Round 1 k6, [k2tog] 6 times, k6: 18 sts
Round 2 knit
Round 3 k3, [kfb] twice, [k2tog] 4 times, [kfb] twice, k3: 18 sts
Round 4 knit
Round 5 k3, kfb, k2, kfb, k4, kfb, k2, kfb, k3: 22 sts
Round 6 knit

SHAPE CROWN (short rows)

Row 1 k4, wrap the next st and turn
Row 2 p8, wrap the next st and turn
Row 3 k7, wrap the next st and turn
Row 4 p6, wrap the next st and turn
Row 5 k5, wrap the next st and turn
Row 6 p4, wrap the next st and turn
Row 7 k2 (to beginning of round)

SHAPE FACE (continue working in the round)

Round 1 knit, working wraps with corresponding sts
Round 2 k3, kfb, k4, kfb, k4, kfb, k4, kfb, k3: 26 sts
Rounds 3-5 knit
Round 6 k1, [ssk] twice, k4, ssk, k4, k2tog, k4, [k2tog] twice, k1: 20 sts
Round 7 knit
Round 8 [ssk] twice, k2, ssk, k4, k2tog, k2, [k2tog] twice: 14 sts
Round 9 knit
Round 10 ssk, k1, ssk, k4, k2tog, k1, k2tog: 10 sts
Rounds 11-12 knit

Leaving sts on the needle(s), lightly stuff neck and head.

Round 13 k1, ssk, k4, k2tog, k1: 8 sts

Knit the first 2 sts of the next round; with 4 sts on the top and 4 sts on the bottom, use the Kitchener stitch to graft the nose.

TAIL (worked in the round)

Use JMCO (see Technique 3, p.12) to CO 18.

Round 1 *kfb, k6, kfb, k1, rep from *: 22 sts
Round 2 *kfb, k8, kfb, k1, rep from *: 26 sts
Round 3 *kfb, k10, kfb, k1, rep from *: 30 sts
Round 4 *kfb, k12, kfb, k1, rep from *: 34 sts
Round 5 knit
Round 6 *kfb, k15, kfb, k1, rep from *: 38 sts
Rounds 7-14 knit
Round 15 *k1, ssk, k13, k2tog, k1, rep from *: 34 sts
Round 16 knit
Round 17 k16, wrap the next st and turn; p15, wrap the next st and turn; k15, knit the next st with its wrap; knit to the end of the round
Round 18 knit the first st with its wrap tbls; k15, wrap the next st and turn; p15, wrap the next st and turn; k15, knit the next st with its wrap; knit to the end of the round
Rounds 19-21 rep round 18
Round 22 knit the first st with its wrap; knit to the end of the round
Rounds 23-29 knit
Round 30 *k1, ssk, k11, k2tog, k1, rep from *: 30 sts
Rounds 31-33 knit
Round 34 *k1, ssk, k9, k2tog, k1, rep from *: 26 sts
Rounds 35-37 knit
Round 38 *k1, ssk, k7, k2tog, k1, rep from *: 22 sts
Rounds 39-41 knit
Round 42 *k1, ssk, k5, k2tog, k1, rep from *: 18 sts
Rounds 43-49 knit
Round 50 k2tog around: 9 sts

BO.

Ears (worked flat, make 2)

CO 5.

Rows 1-2 knit
Row 3 ssk, k1, k2tog: 3 sts
Row 4 knit
Row 5 k2tog, k1: 2 sts

BO. Repeat for second ear.

Feet (worked in the round, make 2)

CO 12. Join in a round.

Rounds 1-10 knit
Round 11 k2tog around: 6 sts

Leaving sts on the needle(s), stuff toe.

Break yarn, thread tail through remaining stitches, pull up and weave through.

Repeat for second foot.

Arms (worked in the round, make 2)

CO 9. Join in a round.

Rounds 1-14 knit
Round 15 *k2tog, k1, rep from * around: 6 sts

Break yarn, thread tail through remaining stitches, pull up and weave through.

Repeat for second arm.

Acorn (worked in the round)

With green, CO 6. Join in a round.

Round 1 knit
Round 2 *kfb, k1, rep from * around: 9 sts
Round 3 knit
Round 4 *kfb, k1, kfb, rep from * around: 15 sts
Rounds 5-13 knit

BO. Stuff firmly.

Acorn hat (worked in the round)

With light brown, CO 6. Join in a round.

Round 1 *kfb, k1, rep from * around: 9 sts
Round 2 knit
Round 3 *kfb, k1, kfb, rep from * around: 15 sts
Round 4 knit
Round 5 *k1, kfb, k1, kfb, k1, rep from * around: 21 sts

BO.

Sew hat to top of acorn. With light brown, make a short, twisted cord (see Technique 8, p. 13) and sew to center of hat for stem.

Assembly and finishing

Sew base of tail to back; then tack top of tail, just under curve, to upper back. Sew ears to crown as shown. With black, make French knot eyes. Sew feet to body as shown. Attach acorn to front as shown. Sew arms in place as shown and tack paws to acorn.

Thank you

Visionary Author friends
for your support and encouragement from the start.

Peggy Jo Wells, Brown Sheep Company, Inc.,
for generously supplying the beautiful yarns used in the samples in this book.

Katherine Bates, artist,
for lovingly creating illustrations of the embroidery stitches.

Amy Polcyn, technical editor,
for turning my patterns into a correct and consistent body of work.

Janel Laidman, designer,
for a lively and fun book design that captures my vision perfectly.

John, my best friend,
for your unshakable belief in me.